In May, 2009, The Chef's Academy suffered a great loss with the passing of Chef Joseph Allford.

We dedicate *Cooking with The Chef's Academy* to his memory and hope that it inspires your creative side, as he inspired us to be creative every day.

cooking with the CHEF'S ACADEMY

PERFORM LIKE A CHEF WITH RECIPES & LESSONS FROM
THE CLASSROOM TO YOUR KITCHEN

Published by Northstar Media Books

Editor Casey Kenley
Art Direction and Design Ashlie Wilson
Photographer Stacy Newgent
Food Stylist Chef Patrick Whetstone
Special Production Matthew Kiefer

Text copyright 2009 by
The Chef's Academy

Photography copyright 2009 by Northstar
Media, LLC d/b/a
Indianapolis dine magazine

All rights reserved. No part of this book may
be reproduced in any form without written
permission from the publisher.

Library of Congress Catalog-in-Publication Data
available.

ISBN-13: 978-0-9820296-5-7

Manufactured in China

10 9 8 7 6 5 4 3 2 1

Northstar Media, LLC
120 East Vermont Street
Indianapolis, IN 46204

thechefsacademy.com
northstarmediabooks.com

table of contents

FOREWORD, 6

Chef Jeffrey Bane, 8
APPETIZERS, 9
Roasted Kohlrabi with Red and Yellow Beets, 11
Bacalao with Aïoli, 12
Cazuela de Pollo con Chorizo y Hongos, 13
Crispelle (Tiny Fried Pizza), 15
Hummus, 16
Jalapeño Pesto, 17
Mint and Pistachio Pesto, 18
Sun-Dried Tomato Tapenade, 19
Chipotle Lime Salsa, 20
Mango Salsa, 21

Chef Scott Bright, 22
SALADS, 23
Green Bean and Fontina Salad, 25
Baby Octopus Salad, 27
Spanish Seafood Salad, 28
Grilled Vegetable Salad, 29

Chef Robert Frye, 30
SOUPS, 31
Cool, Refreshing Rhubarb Soup, 32
Gazpacho Blanco, 33
Corn Chowder, 35
Provençal White Bean Soup, 36

Pumpkin Velouté with Serrano Ham and Dates, 37
Beer and Cheddar Soup, 38
Estofado de Conejo (Rabbit Stew), 39

Chef Matthew Mejía, 40
VEGETABLES & SEAFOOD, 41
Stuffed Peppers with Tomato Vinaigrette, 43
Egg Pasta Dough, 44
Sun-Dried Tomato Mushroom Ravioli, 45
Roasted Portobello and Spinach Couscous Wrap, 46
English Claiborne, 47
Paddlefish Fajitas, 49
Grilled Swordfish with Tabasco Anchovy Sauce and Sun-Dried Tomatoes, 50
Saffron Mussels with Ham, Peppers and Tomatoes, 51
Rock Shrimp (Langoustines) with Tarragon Cream Sauce, 53

Chef Anthony G. Hanslits, 54
POULTRY & PORK, 55
Spicy Chicken Kebabs, 57
Chicken Tagine, 59
Duck Ragu and Sweet Corn "Risotto," 61
Pork Medallions with Marsala, Garlic and Herbs, 62
Garlic Herb-Encrusted Pork Loin, 63
Butter "Poached" Pork Loin with Warm Onion Marmalade, 65

Chef Lucas Trinosky, 66
LAMB & BEEF, 67
Lamb Fricassee, 69
Veal Scaloppini with Mozzarella, 70
Filet of Beef with Oregano and Garlic Olive Oil, 71
Butter-Burgers, 73

Chef Joseph Allford, 74
DESSERTS, 75
Coconut Flan, 77
Cake and Ice Cream, 78
Pear and Persimmon Tart, 80
Sweet Potato Tart, 81
Chocolate Soufflé with Crème Anglaise, 83

Chef Pierre Giacometti, 84
BREADS, 85
Apple Brioche, 87
Raisin Bread, 88
Mediterranean Olive Bread, 89
Three-Strand Braids, 90
Fresh Whole Wheat Pita Bread, 91

INDEX, 92

foreword.

My career as a chef has given me the opportunity to eat and cook in some extraordinary places and meet interesting people from all walks of life. I truly believed that when I left the everyday grind of the professional kitchen that I would use that free time to give back to the community and to my beloved food industry. After 36 years, that time arrived. My pace was a little slower, my body ached more than usual and my patience was not as forgiving as it used to be. It was time to pass the torch to a new generation of chefs.

The Chef's Academy is building knowledge and passion in the culinary industry every day. The students who pass through our halls have an enthusiasm that is necessary to succeed in this business. That determination is combined with qualities that make each student special in his or her own way, whether it's a doggedness to excel, the ability to overcome tough circumstances or a raw talent for cooking. We are helping all of these students build not only careers in the food industry, but also strength of character that will influence them in every aspect of their lives.

As Dean of Culinary Education, I am proud to acknowledge all the talent and experiences that our chefs and instructors bring to this facility and the entire community. With that in mind, we present *Cooking with The Chef's Academy*, a collection of 50 recipes from our Chef Instructors for home cooks. With a nod to education, we have included techniques, tips and tidbits with many of these dishes to teach you some of the tricks of the trade. As you read and administer the recipes in *Cooking with The Chef's Academy*, remember all the time and effort these gifted chefs and instructors are passing on to future chefs. We all teach from the heart. Sometimes we may be a little rough, but it is all for the benefit of the student.

There are many people who make The Chef's Academy a success. Behind the scenes, everyone from the admissions, financial aid and administrative departments play very important roles in molding our students. It really takes a village to raise a chef. A special thanks goes to Harrison College's Ken Konesco, who had a vision of bringing culinary education to a different level in Indianapolis and for Regional Director Jayson Boyers, who guides us on this journey.

Learn much and eat well,

chef jeffrey bane.

Chef Jeffrey Bane's career in professional kitchens illustrates how cooking can land you in some incredible destinations. He was born and raised in northern Indiana and after high school enrolled at Johnson & Wales University in Charleston, from where he received an Associate's Degree in Culinary Arts and a Bachelor's Degree in Food Service Management. From there, he completed an externship at The Breakers Palm Beach resort, an inveterate winner of the coveted AAA Five Diamond Award.

Deciding to travel west for a little adventure, Bane began what would become more than a decade of seasonal resort executive chef experience. Soaking up the views and honing his culinary skills, he worked in some of the most popular ski resorts and national parks in the United States, including Deer Valley Resort in Park City, Utah, and Glacier National Park in Montana, where he was the corporate executive chef and coordinated seven properties. Resorts in New Zealand, France and Austria followed as he spent three years overseas, including a season in the Balearic Islands of Spain as a private chef.

Upon returning to the United States, Bane traveled far north to work during the summer months as executive chef for the Grande Denali Lodge and for Princess Alaska Hotels and Lodges. He and his wife spent their last ski season in Sun Valley, Idaho, where he was chef for the Trail Creek Cabin, a cozy backcountry restaurant built in 1937 and known as a former haunt of Ernest Hemingway.

Moving back home to Indiana, Bane accepted the executive chef position at The Oakwood Inn and Conference Center on Lake Wawasee before becoming a full-time Chef Instructor at The Chef's Academy. He obtained an Associate in Applied Science degree in Pastry Arts from TCA in 2008. He is a Certified ServSafe Instructor and exam proctor. He is also a National Ice Carving Association Certified Ice Carver and since 2003 has received many medals in related events throughout the Midwest. He placed sixth in the professional category in the 2008 Nationals Competition in Chicago. Bane also received the Superior Chef award at Indiana Pork's Taste of Elegance competition in 2008.

appetizers

roasted kohlrabi with red and yellow beets

BY CHEF JEFFREY BANE

5 large red and yellow beets
3 kohlrabi, trimmed
Melted butter, as needed, to taste
Kosher salt, to taste
Freshly ground black pepper, to taste
Wine, stock or water, for reheating

1. Preheat oven to 350 degrees. Peel the beets and kohlrabi and coat them with butter. Season with salt and pepper, to taste.

2. Individually wrap each vegetable in aluminum foil and roast in the 350-degree oven until tender (about 1 hour).

3. Unwrap the vegetables and allow them to cool. Slice or dice according to your liking.

4. Reheat them in a shallow pan with a bit of liquid such as wine, stock or even water. The liquid should evaporate as the beets are heated through. Coat and season with butter, salt and pepper, to taste.

Serves 6-8

bacalao with aïoli

BY CHEF ROBERT FRYE

1 head garlic
Olive oil, for drizzling
1½ cups mayonnaise
5 pounds salt cod, soaked overnight, bones and skin removed
1½ pounds Yukon gold potatoes, peeled
Kosher salt, to taste
2 tablespoons chopped parsley
Freshly ground black pepper, to taste
About 1 quart vegetable oil, for deep-frying
2 eggs, beaten
2 cups bread crumbs

1. Preheat oven to 350 degrees.

2. Chop the top off of the garlic bulb. Drizzle the head and exposed cloves with olive oil and wrap the entire head in foil. Bake the garlic in the 350-degree oven until it is soft (45–50 minutes).

3. To make the aïoli, squeeze the roasted garlic from the cloves and blend with the mayonnaise; reserve.

4. Flake all of the salt cod and reserve.

5. Boil the potatoes in lightly salted water until soft. Drain well. Break them apart in a stand mixer, with the back of a fork or with a potato masher until mushy. Mix in the parsley and season with salt and pepper, to taste.

6. Fold together the potato mixture and salt cod. Form the mixture into balls about 3 ounces each (big enough to fit in the palm of your hand). (The starch in the potatoes will help hold them together; if they seem a little dry, you may add a small amount of milk or olive oil to smooth them out.)

7. Heat the oil over medium-high heat to 360 degrees using a candy thermometer. Roll the balls in the eggs and then in the bread crumbs. Deep-fry them until golden brown. Remove to kitchen paper.

8. Serve the bacalao balls with the aïoli.

Yields 12 balls

cazuela de pollo con chorizo y hongos

BY CHEF MATTHEW MEJÍA

- 2 tablespoons olive oil
- 1 pound chicken breast meat, cut into ¼-inch dice
- Kosher salt, to taste
- Freshly ground black pepper, to taste
- 4 ounces chorizo sausage, cut into ¼-inch dice
- ¼ cup chopped onion
- 1 tablespoon chopped garlic
- ¼ cup sliced crimini mushrooms
- 1 tablespoon chopped fresh thyme, plus more to garnish
- 1 tablespoon chopped fresh parsley, plus more to garnish
- 1 cup chicken stock
- ¼ cup dry white wine (Albariño, Viura, Sauvignon Blanc)

1. Into a saute pan over medium heat, pour the oil. Season the chicken pieces with salt and pepper, to taste. When the oil is hot, add the chicken and saute 2–3 minutes, stirring constantly for even browning.

2. Add the chorizo sausage and saute for 2 minutes. Add the onion, garlic, mushrooms, thyme and parsley and saute for 5 minutes. Add the stock and white wine and simmer for 2 more minutes.

3. Garnish with the additional chopped thyme and parsley to serve as an appetizer or as part of a tapas menu.

Serves 4–6

crispelle (tiny fried pizza)

BY CHEF LUCAS TRINOSKY

1 pound unbaked frozen pizza/bread dough divided into 4 4-ounce pieces
Vegetable oil, for frying
Kosher salt, to taste
Freshly ground black pepper, to taste
¼ cup extra-virgin olive oil
¼ ounce basil, leaves torn (about 15 leaves)
3-4 Roma tomatoes, sliced ¼-inch thick
4 ounces cooked shrimp, shelled and deveined
3-4 ounces Parmesan cheese, grated (½ cup grated cheese)
2-4 ounces prosciutto, very thinly sliced
2 ounces chopped olives

1. Roll out the 4 pieces of dough into 6- to 8-inch pizza shapes.
2. Heat the vegetable oil in a pan over medium-high heat. Panfry each pizza crust in hot oil until it is golden and cooked through (5-10 minutes, depending on thickness). Remove from the oil and drain on paper towels; season immediately with a little salt and pepper, to taste.
3. Preheat oven to 375 degrees.
4. Place the 4 crusts on a cookie sheet and drizzle 1 tablespoon olive oil on each one. Arrange the torn basil leaves on each shell. Add the sliced tomatoes and cooked shrimp. Season with a little salt and pepper, to taste.
5. Finish with the Parmesan cheese. Bake in the 375-degree oven until the cheese is melted (5-10 minutes).
6. Remove from the oven, add the prosciutto and sprinkle with olives.
7. Cut and serve while hot.

Serves 4

hummus

BY CHEF ANTHONY G. HANSLITS

2 15-ounce cans chickpeas, rinsed and drained
¾ cup water
½ cup tahini paste
¼-⅓ cup fresh lemon juice, to taste
½ tablespoon kosher salt
3 cloves garlic
½ teaspoon freshly ground black pepper, or to taste
¼ teaspoon cayenne pepper
½ teaspoon chili powder
1 teaspoon ground cumin
¼ cup olive oil

1. In a food processor, combine the chickpeas, water, tahini paste, lemon juice, salt, garlic, black pepper, cayenne pepper, chili powder and cumin; puree.
2. While the motor is running, pour in the olive oil and process until fully incorporated. Season with pepper, to taste. Serve with pita wedges, crusty bread or celery sticks.

Yields about 2½ cups

jalapeño pesto

BY CHEF ANTHONY G. HANSLITS

10 jalapeños, halved lengthwise and seeded
6 cloves garlic
½ cup pine nuts, toasted (see technique on page 18)
½ cup olive oil
1 cup grated Parmesan cheese

1. Place all of the ingredients in a food processor and blend well. Be careful to avoid overprocessing. It should not be perfectly smooth; the pesto should have some body.
2. Serve with grilled pork chops or chicken.

Yields 2½ cups

mint and pistachio pesto

BY CHEF ANTHONY G. HANSLITS

1 tightly packed cup fresh mint leaves
Kosher salt, to taste
2 cloves garlic
2 tablespoons extra-virgin olive oil
3 tablespoons grated Parmesan cheese
2 tablespoons grated Pecorino cheese
3 tablespoons unsalted pistachios

1. Combine the mint with a little salt, to taste, in a food processor and process a few seconds until chopped.

2. Add the garlic and half of the olive oil. Continue to process, adding the cheeses and the rest of the olive oil. Process until a smooth sauce is formed. Add the pistachios and process until the nuts are well broken up, but do not completely grind them.

3. Serve this pesto with grilled lamb, potato gnocchi or as a dipping sauce.

Yields 1 cup

technique.

If you prefer a richer nut flavor, toast the pistachios first. To toast most any nut, simply place them on a sheet pan or in a heavy skillet and cook using moderate heat until golden brown.

sun-dried tomato tapenade

BY CHEF ANTHONY G. HANSLITS

½ cup sun-dried tomatoes
2 tablespoons capers
1 cup pitted kalamata olives
2 cloves garlic, peeled
½ teaspoon lemon juice
¼ cup extra-virgin olive oil
2 tablespoons fresh rosemary leaves
¼ cup water

1. Combine all of the ingredients in a food processor and process until smooth.
2. Serve on crostini or endive leaves.

Yields 2¼ cups

chipotle lime salsa

5 large tomatoes, diced
4 cloves garlic, chopped
4 chipotle peppers, reconstituted and chopped
½ red onion, finely diced
¼ cup finely chopped cilantro
Juice of 2 limes, adding lime zest as well if you want
Kosher salt, to taste
Freshly ground black pepper, to taste

1. Combine all of the ingredients and let the mixture sit at room temperature for at least 30 minutes.
2. Serve with grilled pita bread.

Yields 3 cups

technique.
To reconstitute chili peppers, soak them in about 2 cups of cold water for 1 hour or until they become tender and appear as they would have before being dried.

mango salsa

**4 ripe mangos, peeled and diced
½ red onion, finely diced
¼ cup finely chopped cilantro
2 jalapeños, seeded and chopped
Juice of 1 lime
Kosher salt, to taste
Freshly ground black pepper, to taste**

1 Combine all of the ingredients and let them sit at room temperature for at least 30 minutes.
2 Serve with grilled pita bread.

Yields 3 cups

technique.
To cut a mango, trim the top and bottom to create a flat, steady base. Peel the fruit by slicing down each side. The wide, flat seed runs the length of the mango. Determine where the seed is and slice down and around it.

chef scott bright.

Chef Scott Bright has been an instructor at The Chef's Academy since its doors opened. He brings with him a wealth of experiences from both professional kitchens and classrooms. His own formal education began at the prestigious Culinary Institute of America, where he received a scholarship based on academic achievement and earned an Associate's of Applied Science Degree in Culinary Arts.

For Last Minute Gourmet, a premier full-service caterer in Chicago serving about 6,000 meals per day, Bright worked as executive chef. He also participated in the high-profile Taste of Chicago event, where he received top accolades. Getting his start as a teacher, Bright taught cooking classes for the Latin School of America and at the Last Minute Gourmet facilities. Moving to the East Coast, Bright worked for the No. 1 catering company in the Hudson Valley, where events included large, high-end fundraisers for top politicians.

In a more intimate setting, Bright worked as a personal chef for families in Carmel and Geist near Indianapolis and provided entertainment-style cooking in peoples' homes. Through Raving Café, Bright owned and operated four separate businesses: a catering facility, restaurant, personal chef service and provider of in-home culinary instruction.

Now as a full-time instructor, Bright collaborates with his colleagues to guide TCA's curriculum and works on a committee to ensure the materials and recipes that students use stay current and relevant in the industry. He is also a Certified ServSafe Instructor. Under his leadership, the school's annual Chili Cook-Off has grown exponentially from an internal tasting to a community outreach opportunity, offering the general public samples of students' best chili recipes. Bright is known for working one-on-one with aspiring chefs and conveying his passion for culinary arts every day. Watching his students succeed in school and in the industry, he says, are his favorite aspects of teaching.

salads

green bean and fontina salad

BY CHEF LUCAS TRINOSKY

Blood Orange Vinaigrette
Juice and zest of 1½ blood oranges
¼ cup extra-virgin olive oil
2 tablespoons canola oil
2 tablespoons red wine vinegar
1 tablespoon sugar
2 teaspoons mint chiffonade, plus more whole leaves to garnish
2 teaspoons tarragon chiffonade, plus more whole leaves to garnish
2 teaspoons basil chiffonade, plus more whole leaves to garnish
Kosher salt, to taste
Freshly ground black pepper, to taste

Salad
Kosher salt, to taste
12 ounces green beans
5 ounces fontina, ⅓-inch julienne (see technique on page 50)
1 medium-size red pepper, ⅓-inch julienne
1 medium-size yellow pepper, ⅓-inch julienne
¾ cup Blood Orange Vinaigrette (recipe above)
3 blood oranges

Blood Orange Vinaigrette
[1] Whisk together all of the dressing ingredients and reserve.

Salad
[1] Bring a pot of salted water to a boil over high heat. Trim the green beans and drop them into the boiling water to blanch (7–10 minutes). Drain and then refresh in ice water; drain well and dry.
[2] Toss together the beans, cheese, peppers and vinaigrette. Chill the salad, allowing it to marinate 45 minutes.
[3] Zest the blood oranges and then peel and slice them. To plate, arrange the orange slices as a base, place the salad in the middle and garnish with the zest and whole herbs.

Serves 4–6

technique.
Cutting greens and herbs into chiffonade allows you to maintain consistency in the width of the pieces and reduces the potential for bruising. Simply roll up the leaves like a cigar and slice across, producing wispy, narrow ribbons.

tip.
The best way to slice soft cheese such as fontina is to cut into it right out of the refrigerator when it's still cold and somewhat firm.

baby octopus salad

BY CHEF ANTHONY G. HANSLITS

Salad
4 quarts water
1 medium-size onion, peeled and quartered
2 stalks celery, cut into 2-inch pieces
1 carrot, peeled and cut into 2-inch pieces
2 bay leaves
12 whole black peppercorns
¾ teaspoon saffron threads
1 tablespoon sea salt
4 pounds baby octopus, beaks removed and discarded, cut in half lengthwise

Dressing
½ cup lemon juice
1 cup extra-virgin olive oil
1 cup peeled and finely diced red onion
1 cup finely diced celery
12 basil leaves, torn
½ teaspoon red pepper flakes
1½ teaspoons sea salt

1. In a large pot, bring the water, onion, celery, carrot, bay leaves, peppercorns, saffron and salt to a simmer over high heat. Reduce heat and continue to simmer the cooking broth for 15 minutes.

2. Prepare an ice water bath large enough to hold a strainer. Add the octopus to the cooking broth and cook for 1 minute and 15 seconds. Remove the octopus from the broth and place in it the strainer; submerge the strainer in the ice water bath. Discard the vegetables and broth.

3. To make the dressing, in a mixing bowl, whisk together the lemon juice and olive oil. Add all of the other dressing ingredients and mix well.

4. Remove the octopus from the ice water bath and place it in a large mixing bowl. Add enough dressing to thoroughly coat the octopus.

5. Serve with Italian country bread brushed with extra-virgin olive oil, sprinkled with a few grinds of sea salt and grilled.

Serves 16

spanish seafood salad

¼ cup Spanish olive oil, or as needed
½ red onion, minced
½ cup peeled, seeded and diced roasted red peppers (see technique on page 43)
1 medium-size tomato, concassée*
2 tablespoons capers
2 cloves garlic, minced
Kosher salt, to taste
½ pound bay scallops
½ pound lump crabmeat (cooked)

½ pound smoked salmon, sliced into strips
Juice of 1 lime
¼ cup oloroso sherry
1 teaspoon ground cumin
2 tablespoons chopped basil
Freshly ground black pepper, to taste
4 cups organic baby greens, or as needed

technique.
Blanching involves immersing an ingredient in a boiling liquid for a short period of time and usually transferring it quickly to an ice water bath to stop the cooking process.

1. Drizzle about 2 tablespoons of the olive oil into a pan over medium heat. Saute the onion, red peppers, tomato, capers and garlic in the oil until the onion is translucent. Remove from heat, transfer to a bowl and chill the mixture in the refrigerator for 15 minutes.

2. Prepare an ice water bath. Bring a pot of salted water to a boil and blanch the scallops until cooked through (2–3 minutes). Drain and plunge the scallops in the ice water bath to stop the cooking.

3. Toss all of the ingredients together (remaining olive oil, sauteed vegetables, seafood and seasonings) except for the greens, and then season with salt and pepper, to taste.

4. Serve the salad on a bed of organic baby greens.

Serves 6

*Concassée is a mixture that is coarsely chopped or ground. For tomato concassée, peel, seed and chop the tomatoes (The New Food Lover's Companion, Third Edition, by Sharon Tyler Herbst).

grilled vegetable salad

BY CHEF ANTHONY G. HANSLITS

Kosher salt, to taste
2 potatoes, cut into ¼-inch wedges
¼ cup extra-virgin olive oil, plus more to taste
Freshly ground black pepper, to taste
1 red bell pepper, cut into ¼-inch strips
1 yellow bell pepper, cut into ¼-inch strips
1 green bell pepper, cut into ¼-inch strips
1 red onion, cut into ¼-inch wedges
2 plum tomatoes, quartered
12 basil leaves, torn

1. Preheat grill to 425 degrees or medium-high heat.
2. Bring a pot of salted water to a boil over high heat. Drop the potato wedges into the boiling water to blanch just until they're 75 percent cooked (still firm but softened) (about 5 minutes). Drain and then refresh the potatoes in ice water; drain well and dry.
3. In a mixing bowl large enough to hold all of the vegetables, mix the olive oil, salt and pepper, to taste. Add all of the vegetables and toss to coat.
4. Grill the vegetables until tender (5–7 minutes). Place them back in the bowl and season with the basil; add more oil, salt and pepper, to taste.

Serves 4

chef robert frye.

Growing up Elwood, Indiana, Chef Robert Frye had always been interested in pursuing a career that combined creativity and imagination. With these attributes in full force and a demanding pace to boot, his aptitude for cooking was given a clear direction. Frye graduated from the Western Culinary Institute in Portland, Oregon, with a diploma from its Le Cordon Bleu Culinary Arts program.

While at school, Frye worked at the prestigious Avalon restaurant in what is now the Avalon Hotel and Spa, honing his skills in French techniques with Asian influences. Under the tutelage of Chef Fernando Davina, he interned at Fiddlehead's, which was crowned Restaurant of the Year by *The Oregonian* while he was there.

Upon graduation, Frye worked at various restaurants. He served as the executive sous chef for The Dundee Bistro in Oregon's Willamette Valley for three years and was the executive chef for Vera Mae's Bistro in Muncie, Indiana. He also owned his own restaurant in Muncie called The Spot. Started as a local diner, the business evolved into an intimate New American–focused restaurant. Most recently, Frye served as the executive chef for Stone Creek Dining Company in Greenwood, Indiana.

Frye joined The Chef's Academy in 2007 as a Chef Instructor. As a teacher, he says he enjoys the personal and professional growth and the chance to positively affect students' lives every day. He teaches kitchen classes as well as food services classes in public relations, personnel management and entrepreneurship. In addition to his regular classes, Frye teaches Saturday community classes and team-building events that TCA offers to area corporations.

soups

cool, refreshing rhubarb soup

2 cups plus 2 tablespoons water
2 cups ¼-inch-dice fresh rhubarb
  (about 3 stalks)
½ cup sugar
1 stick cinnamon
2 tablespoons cornstarch
½ cup heavy cream, to garnish

1. Bring the 2 cups water to a boil in a saucepan over high heat. Stir in the rhubarb, sugar and cinnamon stick. Reduce the heat to a simmer and cover, cooking until the rhubarb is very tender (about 15 minutes).
2. In a small bowl, mix together the cornstarch and 2 tablespoons water. Slowly add this to the saucepan, stirring it into the soup.
3. Increase heat and continue to stir until the soup boils for a few more minutes; the soup will be translucent and thick.
4. Remove the cinnamon stick and transfer the soup to a large bowl. Allow it to cool and then cover and chill it in the refrigerator.
5. When you're ready to serve the soup, whip the cream into medium peaks. Ladle the soup into bowls and float several whip cream puffs on top.

Serves 4

gazpacho blanco

8 ounces seedless white grapes, plus more to garnish
1 large cucumber, seeded and chopped
1 shallot, chopped
1 clove garlic, minced
2 cups plain yogurt (low fat is fine)
Kosher salt, to taste
Freshly ground black pepper, to taste
8 drops hot pepper sauce, or to taste
Toasted sliced almonds, to garnish (see technique on page 18)

1. Puree the grapes in a blender. Strain and return the juice to the blender.
2. Add the cucumber, shallot and garlic and puree until smooth.
3. Blend in the yogurt.
4. Season with salt, pepper and hot pepper sauce, to taste. Cover and chill.
5. Halve the additional white grapes, to garnish. Top bowls of soup with the grapes and almonds and serve cold.

Serves 2–3

corn chowder

BY CHEF ANTHONY G. HANSLITS

8 cups chicken broth
4 ounces (1 stick) butter
4 ounces pancetta or bacon, diced
1 cup diced red onion
1 cup diced yellow onion
½ cup diced celery
1 red pepper, seeded and diced
1 yellow pepper, seeded and diced
3 bay leaves
8 ears corn, kernels cut from the cob
½ cup flour
4 cups skin-on, diced potatoes (red or baking potato)
2 cups heavy cream
Kosher salt, to taste
Freshly ground black pepper, to taste

1. In a large saucepan, warm up the broth over medium-low heat.
2. In a large soup pot, melt the butter and then add the pancetta or bacon. Cook until the meat starts to turn light brown.
3. Add the onions, celery, peppers, bay leaves and corn; cook until the onions are translucent.
4. Stir in the flour and cook 3-4 minutes.
5. Add the warm broth and stir to incorporate the vegetable mixture; bring to a simmer. Continue to cook for 20 minutes and then add the potatoes. Simmer until the potatoes are just tender.
6. Add the cream and then season, to taste, with salt and pepper.

Serves 8-10

tidbit.

Indiana ranks fifth in the nation for the production of grain corn used as livestock feed, sweeteners, alternative energies and more. Corn was the leading source of income for Indiana farmers in 2007, amounting to $2.71 billion in cash receipts, according to the U.S. Department of Agriculture. While sweet corn isn't our bread and butter, it wouldn't be summer in Indiana without it on the table.

provençal white bean soup
BY CHEF ROBERT FRYE

Pistou
10 cloves garlic
2 bunches fresh basil
1 tablespoon coarse salt
1½ cups grated Parmesan cheese
2 cups peeled, diced tomatoes
1 cup extra-virgin olive oil

Soup
1½ cups dried white beans
3 leeks, white and light green parts only, small dice
1 yellow onion, diced
3 carrots, diced
½ cup extra-virgin olive oil
3 medium-size zucchini, diced
3 quarts chicken stock
½ pound green beans
Kosher salt, to taste
1 cup dried pasta such as farfalle or orzo

Pistou
1. Blend all of the ingredients except for the oil in a food processor to form a paste. Drizzle in the oil and stir gently to combine (it should be quite loose).
2. Set aside or store until service.

Soup
1. Soak the white beans in water overnight.
2. Drain the beans and then cover them with fresh water in a saucepan. Simmer on the stovetop until they are tender (30–45 minutes).
3. In a heavy-bottomed stockpot, sweat the leeks, onion and carrots in the olive oil over medium heat until the carrots are tender. Add the remaining ingredients except for the pasta, seasoning with salt, to taste; simmer until the green beans are tender.
4. Cook the pasta in boiling, salted water until al dente. Drain well.
5. Portion the pasta into serving bowls. Pour the soup over the top. Garnish with pistou.

Serves 8–10

pumpkin velouté with serrano ham and dates

BY CHEF ROBERT FRYE

5 ounces serrano ham slices, small dice
3 ounces unsalted butter
1 red onion, finely diced
2 pounds canned pumpkin
3 quarts chicken stock
1 pound russet potatoes, peeled
2 bay leaves
1 sprig fresh rosemary
Kosher salt, to taste
Cayenne pepper, to taste
Nutmeg, to taste
Pitted dates, to garnish

1. Render the ham slices with butter in the bottom of a large, heavy-bottomed stockpot over medium heat. When browned, remove the ham slices and reserve. Add the onion to the pot and cook over medium heat until translucent.

2. Add the pumpkin, stock and potatoes. Wrap the bay leaves and rosemary in cheesecloth, tie to secure and drop into the pot (see technique on page 65). Simmer until the potatoes are fully cooked (30–45 minutes).

3. Season with salt, cayenne pepper and nutmeg, to taste. Remove the herb sachet. Puree the soup until it is smooth and velvety. Strain through a fine-mesh strainer.

4. To serve, garnish with the reserved ham and dates.

Serves 8–10

beer and cheddar soup

BY CHEF ANTHONY G. HANSLITS

4 ounces (1 stick) butter
1 medium-size onion, diced
½ cup flour
2 cups chicken broth
1 12-ounce beer
¾ pound grated cheddar cheese
Kosher salt and freshly ground black pepper mix, to taste (see tip on page 73)

1. In a casserole over medium heat, melt the butter with the onion, cooking until the onion is translucent. Stir in the flour, making a roux.

2. In a separate pan, bring the broth and beer to a boil. Slowly add the broth mixture to the roux, stirring constantly until all the liquid has been used. Simmer for 20 minutes.

3. Add the cheese, and then season with the salt and pepper mix, to taste. Puree in a blender or use an immersion blender and serve.

Serves 4

estofado de conejo (rabbit stew)

BY CHEF MATTHEW MEJÍA

6 rabbit legs, meat removed from the bones and cubed (reserve bones)
Flour, as needed
Kosher salt, to taste
Freshly ground black pepper, to taste
2 tablespoons olive oil, or as needed
2 large sprigs fresh rosemary, chopped
2 large sprigs fresh thyme, chopped
2 medium-size carrots, diced
2 medium-size onions, diced
2 roasted red peppers, peeled, seeded and diced (see technique on page 43)
4 cloves garlic, minced
4 ounces sliced crimini mushrooms
2 large tomatoes, peeled, seeded and diced (see technique on page 69)
1 cup dry white wine
½ cup dry sherry
1 bunch green onions, chopped, to garnish

1. Place the rabbit bones in a stockpot and cover them with water (at least 2½ pints). Simmer for at least 1 hour to make stock. Reserve.

2. Toss the cubed meat in flour seasoned with salt and pepper. In a large skillet, add about 2 tablespoons olive oil and heat over medium-high heat; brown the meat in the hot oil on all sides.

3. Throw in the rosemary, thyme, carrots, onions, peppers and garlic and sweat for a few minutes.

4. Add the mushrooms and tomatoes and season with salt and pepper, to taste. Cook for a couple more minutes.

5. Deglaze the pan with white wine and dry sherry, scraping up any bits stuck to the bottom of the pan (see technique on page 53). Pour in 2 pints of the reserved stock and simmer over a low flame for at least 1 hour. Season with salt and pepper, to taste, and garnish with green onions. Serve with a smile!

Serves 6–8

chef matthew mejía.

Chef Matthew Mejía was born in Kansas City, Missouri, raised in Carmel, Indiana, and grew up in culinary school. Mejía says that cooking was just a job for him before he realized that he was pretty good at it and that he enjoyed being able to make food that people appreciated. Following his intuition, a formal education was the next step.

After graduating from Joliet Junior College in Illinois with an Associate of Applied Science degree in Culinary Arts, he worked in restaurants, casinos, country clubs and hotels in Illinois, Arizona and Indiana. Mejía's most recent restaurant job was as executive sous chef at the Sheraton Indianapolis Hotel and Suites.

Before joining The Chef's Academy staff, he owned Mejía America, a wine-importing company that concentrated on Spanish varietals. He has studied grape cultivation in Spain, along the West Coast and Switzerland, and he is training to become a certified sommelier. Mejía also recently spent time in Australia studying the culinary industry there as an Indiana delegate through Rotary International's Group Study Exchange program.

As a restaurant consultant, Mejía has developed overall menus, wine menus and tastings, food-preparation systems and food-ordering systems. He has also worked as a full-service caterer and produced a line of spices and nuts for sale at area farmers markets in 2008.

Mejía has been with The Chef's Academy since it opened in September 2006 and has assisted in the development of its curriculum. He has taught all of the kitchen classes offered, the wine and spirits course, as well as other food service topics. Reaching out to Indianapolis residents, Mejía instructs TCA's community classes covering Spanish tapas, Australian wine and food pairing, and summer sauces, and has instructed home cooks in classes at the Indiana State Fair. Developing his own culinary expertise, Chef Mejía is studying butchering, ice carving, cheese making, pastry arts and molecular gastronomy.

stuffed peppers with tomato vinaigrette

BY CHEF ANTHONY G. HANSLITS

Tomato Vinaigrette

½ cup skinned, seeded and finely chopped tomatoes (see technique on page 69)
1 shallot, finely chopped
2 tablespoons chopped basil
¼ cup white wine vinegar
½ cup olive oil
Kosher salt, to taste
Freshly ground black pepper, to taste

Stuffed Peppers

4 red bell peppers, roasted
½ cup bread crumbs
2 tablespoons red wine vinegar
2 tablespoons extra-virgin olive oil
½ cup diced yellow bell pepper
1 cup diced eggplant
¼ cup diced green onions
½ cup diced zucchini
1 clove garlic, sliced
½ cup grated provolone cheese
1 large egg, whisked
1 tablespoon minced oregano
1 tablespoon minced Italian parsley
1 tablespoon minced basil
Kosher salt, to taste
Freshly ground black pepper, to taste

Tomato Vinaigrette

[1] Place all of the ingredients in a mixing bowl and combine well. Set aside.

Stuffed Peppers

[1] Preheat oven to 350 degrees.

[2] Cut the top off of each roasted red pepper. Peel and then remove the ribs and seeds without tearing the meat. Set aside.

[3] Soak the bread crumbs in the vinegar for 5 minutes. Squeeze them dry and set aside.

[4] Heat the olive oil in a deep skillet over medium-high heat. Add the yellow pepper, eggplant and green onions and cook 3-5 minutes. Add the zucchini and garlic and cook for another 5 minutes.

[5] Place the vegetables in a large mixing bowl and add the remaining ingredients, seasoning with salt and pepper, to taste.

[6] Gently stuff the peppers with the vegetable mixture. Place the stuffed peppers on an oiled cookie pan. Bake in the 350-degree oven 20-25 minutes. Cool to room temperature. Serve with the tomato vinaigrette.

Serves 4

technique.

To roast bell peppers, preheat your broiler. Place the peppers on a baking sheet skin side up and broil them until blackened, turning as needed to cook them on all sides (10-12 minutes). Drop them into a plastic, resealable bag and seal, allowing them to stand for 10 minutes to make peeling easier.

egg pasta dough

BY CHEF LUCAS TRINOSKY

¼ teaspoon kosher salt
2 cups all-purpose or durum flour*
3 large eggs
2 tablespoons oil (90 percent olive and 10 percent vegetable oil)

1. In a mixing bowl, combine the salt and flour by hand.
2. In a separate bowl, beat the eggs and oil together with a fork until combined.
3. On a hard, smooth surface, place the flour and salt mix and make a deep well in the center. Pour the egg mixture into the well. Working from the inside out with a fork, form a ball of dough. Place the dough in a stainless-steel bowl, cover with plastic wrap and allow it to rest for 20 minutes.
4. Knead the dough by hand on a lightly floured surface until it is firm and smooth. Cover with plastic wrap and let the dough rest for 15 more minutes.
5. Cut the dough into quarters. For each piece, roll ½-inch thin with a rolling pin into a long oblong piece (do not use flour). With the piece running east to west on the counter, fold the dough inward like a trifold wallet. Roll north to south with the rolling pin to reach ¼-inch thickness.
6. With your pasta maker set at the largest setting, run the dough through. Reduce the pasta maker setting one size each time you run the dough through until you reach your desired thickness.

Yields about 1 pound dough (4 4-ounce portions)

Compared to all-purpose flour, durum flour creates a stronger dough. It has a yellow hue and more protein, which creates a more resilient bond once it's kneaded with a liquid.

vegetables & seafood

sun-dried tomato mushroom ravioli

BY CHEF LUCAS TRINOSKY

2 cups whole mushrooms
½ cup sun-dried tomatoes, minced by hand
1 clove garlic, chopped
3-6 sprigs fresh herbs such as basil, oregano and thyme, chopped
¼ cup minced onion
1 cup white wine
Kosher salt, to taste
Freshly ground black pepper, to taste

1 cup ricotta cheese
½ cup grated Parmesan cheese, plus more to garnish
1 recipe Egg Pasta Dough (see recipe on page 44)

1 Mince the mushrooms in a food processor.

2 Simmer the mushrooms, tomatoes, garlic, about ³/₄ of the herbs and onion in the wine over medium to medium-high heat until most of the liquid is cooked off (10-12 minutes). Season with salt and pepper, to taste, and allow the mixture to cool.

3 Mix in the ricotta and Parmesan.

4 Roll out the egg pasta dough to ¹/₁₀-inch thickness; cut it into 32 rounds or squares about 3 inches in diameter.

5 Moisten the edges of the pasta with water and fill 16 of them with the mushroom mix (about 1 tablespoon each). Cover the filled pasta with the remaining 16 pasta shapes and press out any air; crimp the edges with a fork.

6 Bring a pot of salted water to a boil over high heat. Cook the ravioli until they have floated for 2 minutes, removing them with a slotted spoon to individual bowls. Garnish with Parmesan cheese and the remaining fresh herbs. Serve with your favorite pasta sauce.

Serves 3 people (5 ravioli each)

roasted portobello and spinach couscous wrap

BY CHEF LUCAS TRINOSKY

Roasted Tomatoes

8 Roma tomatoes, halved across
2 tablespoons extra-virgin olive oil
1 tablespoon balsamic vinegar
Chopped herbs such as rosemary, thyme and basil, to taste
Kosher salt, to taste
Freshly ground black pepper, to taste

Marinated Portobello

½ cup extra-virgin olive oil
½ cup balsamic vinegar
¼ cup molasses
¼ cup chopped herbs such as rosemary, thyme and basil
¼ cup honey
4 portobello mushroom caps

Spinach Couscous

4 ounces fresh spinach
1 tablespoon butter
1 cup vegetable stock
1 tablespoon chopped herbs such as rosemary, thyme and basil
Kosher salt, to taste
Freshly ground black pepper, to taste
½ cup couscous

Wrap

4 12- to 16-inch flour tortillas
½ cup cream cheese (plain or a savory blend such as roasted garlic or garden vegetable)

Roasted Tomatoes

1. Preheat oven to 300 degrees.
2. On a jelly roll pan or in a baking dish, toss the tomatoes with the rest of the ingredients.
3. Roast in the 300-degree oven until they are very soft and tender (about 1 hour). Chop and set aside.

Marinated Portobello

1. Mix all of the marinade ingredients together and pour over the caps in a nonreactive container. Allow the mushrooms to marinate 15-20 minutes.
2. Preheat oven to 350 degrees.
3. Remove the caps from the marinade (reserving the remaining marinade to use as an optional dressing to serve) and place them on a sheet pan. Roast in the 350-degree oven until tender (15-20 minutes, depending on size of the cap). Cut into ½-inch slices.

Spinach Couscous

1. Saute the spinach in butter over medium heat just until wilted. Add the stock and herbs. Season with salt and pepper, to taste.
2. Increase heat to medium-high and when the stock comes to a boil, add the couscous; remove from heat and cover. When the liquid has been absorbed, fluff the couscous with a fork and allow it to cool.

Wrap

1. Heat the tortillas in a dry skillet or in the microwave. Spread 2 tablespoons of cream cheese on half of each one.
2. On the other half, spread (to cover completely) portobello slices, spinach couscous and roasted tomatoes.
3. Roll up the tortillas to finish, using the cream cheese to help adhere the wraps; slice in half to serve. You may serve these with a little of the portobello marinade as a dressing.

Serves 4

english claiborne

BY CHEF LUCAS TRINOSKY

Avocado Mixture

½ cup diced avocado
3 tablespoons seeded and diced tomato
½ teaspoon extra-virgin olive oil
Kosher salt, to taste
Freshly ground black pepper, to taste

Seafood

3 tablespoons canola oil
16 shrimp, 16-20 size, peeled, deveined and cut into 3 pieces
4 scallops, U-10 size, quartered into discs
1 cup sliced mushrooms
1 packed cup fresh spinach, cleaned
1 heaping tablespoon minced shallot
1 cup dry white wine
1 teaspoon minced fresh tarragon
¼ cup unsalted butter
Kosher salt, to taste
Freshly ground black pepper, to taste

To plate

2 tablespoons butter
4 English muffins, split

Avocado Mixture

1. Mix all of the ingredients well, being sure not to smash them together.
2. Season, to taste, with salt and pepper. Cover the surface of the avocado mixture with plastic wrap (to keep the avocado from discoloring) and store in a refrigerator.

Seafood

1. Heat a saute pan over medium heat. Add the oil.
2. Add the shrimp and scallops and saute in the hot oil for 1 minute. Add the mushrooms, spinach and shallot. Cook 1-2 more minutes.
3. Deglaze the pan with wine (see technique on page 53) and then add the tarragon. Cook and reduce until au sec (almost dry).
4. Swirl in the butter and then season with salt and pepper, to taste. Set aside.

To plate

1. Butter and grill the muffin halves, or toast and butter them. Shingle 2 halves in the center of each plate.
2. Neatly pour the seafood on top.
3. Garnish with the avocado mixture.

Serves 4

48 | vegetables & seafood

paddlefish fajitas

BY CHEF MATTHEW MEJÍA

Paddlefish

1. In a nonreactive container, make a marinade by combining all of the ingredients except for the paddlefish.
2. Add the julienned paddlefish to the mixture and let it marinate at least 30 minutes and up to 1 hour.

Guacamole

1. Mash the avocado meat with the rest of the ingredients. Season with salt and Tabasco sauce, to taste. Reserve until time to serve.

To serve

1. Saute the onions and peppers in vegetable oil over medium-high heat until the onions become translucent.
2. Add the paddlefish, drained of the marinade, and saute until the fish is cooked through.
3. Drizzle a little oil in a separate pan and heat up the tortillas until they bubble.
4. Fill the tortillas with the paddlefish and veggies and top with your favorite condiments such as Monterey Jack cheese, sour cream and guacamole.

Serves 4–6

Paddlefish
Juice of 4 limes
½ cup extra-virgin olive oil
2 teaspoons chopped oregano
2 teaspoons freshly ground black pepper
2 teaspoons kosher salt
1 teaspoon freshly ground cumin
1 clove garlic, minced or 1 teaspoon minced garlic
½ packed cup cilantro
2 pounds paddlefish or other fresh fish, cut into French fry-size julienne (see technique on page 50)

Guacamole
4 avocadoes
½ cup diced Bermuda onion
1 tomato, seeded and diced
4 tablespoons lime juice
Kosher salt, to taste
Tabasco sauce, to taste

To serve
2-3 yellow onions, halved and then sliced
1-2 bell peppers, julienned
Vegetable oil, as needed
12 flour or corn tortillas (2-3 per person)
Shredded Monterey Jack cheese, to serve
Sour cream, to serve

grilled swordfish with tabasco anchovy sauce and sun-dried tomatoes

BY CHEF SCOTT BRIGHT

Israeli Couscous

1 cup water
1 tablespoon extra-virgin olive oil
½ cup couscous
¼ cup thinly sliced celery
1 pinch salt
1 pinch pepper

Swordfish

3 tablespoons extra-virgin olive oil, plus more as needed
2 tablespoons small-dice onion
1 teaspoon minced garlic
2 teaspoons minced anchovy filets
1 teaspoon fresh thyme
½ cup dry white wine
½ teaspoon Tabasco red pepper sauce
¼ cup sun-dried tomatoes, julienned
2 swordfish steaks
12 celery leaves
Juice from ½ lemon
Kosher salt, to taste
Freshly ground black pepper, to taste

Israeli Couscous

1. Bring the water and oil to a boil in a saucepot.
2. Stir in the couscous, celery, salt and pepper. Cook over low heat for about 3 minutes.
3. Remove from heat and let stand until the water is absorbed. Keep warm until service.

Swordfish

1. Place a saucepan on high heat. Add the 3 tablespoons olive oil and onion, sauteing until browned edges appear. Add the garlic and anchovies, stirring well and then immediately adding the thyme, wine, Tabasco sauce and sun-dried tomatoes. Set the sauce aside.
2. Preheat grill to high heat. Lightly coat the fish with olive oil.
3. Grill the swordfish until desired doneness is achieved (130 degrees internal temperature for medium-rare). The meat should be moist, white and firm.
4. Just before serving, stir the celery leaves and lemon juice into the sauce. Season with salt and pepper, to taste, and drizzle over the swordfish. Serve with the couscous.

Serves 2

technique.

A directive for "julienne" typically calls for cutting an ingredient into ⅓-inch-square sticks or thinner. When cutting fresh vegetables such as potatoes or zucchini, slice off the ends to create a flat base for stability. Cut evenly across the ingredient to create long, uniform sticks.

saffron mussels with ham, peppers and tomatoes

BY CHEF MATTHEW MEJIA

1 pinch saffron threads, crumbled
¼ cup dry white wine
3 tablespoons extra-virgin olive oil
2 pounds fresh mussels, cleaned
2 ounces smoked ham, thickly sliced and then diced (standard bacon or jowl bacon is also good)
1 onion, minced
2 cloves garlic, minced
2 tablespoons chopped rosemary
¼ cup fish or shellfish stock
½ red bell pepper, finely chopped
½ green bell pepper, finely chopped
2 medium-size tomatoes, diced

tidbit.

A "stock" refers to a broth kept on hand to make soups or sauces. Cooking poultry, meat, seafood or vegetables in water, often with additional flavorings such as herbs or other vegetables, and then straining the liquid creates this basic soup or broth.

1. Soak the crumbled saffron in the wine for 15 minutes.
2. While the saffron is soaking, in a large pot, heat the olive oil over high heat until just smoking. Add the cleaned mussels and saute them in the hot oil until they just begin to open. Add the ham and saute for 1 minute.
3. Add the onion, garlic and rosemary and saute for 2 more minutes, reducing heat as needed to prevent burning the vegetables.
4. Add the white wine with the saffron and the stock. Stir to combine.
5. Add the peppers and tomatoes; cover for about 3 minutes or until the mussels are completely open. Serve immediately.

Serves 4

tidbit.

Saffron is the world's most expensive, readily available herb. The delicate threads are the stigma from a species of crocus and must be harvested by hand. In culinary uses, it imparts a somewhat bitter, hay-like flavor and a bold yellow hue.

rock shrimp (langoustines) with tarragon cream sauce

BY CHEF MATTHEW MEJÍA

1 pound rock shrimp, peeled and deveined
2 tablespoons clarified butter
2 cloves garlic, minced
1 shallot, minced
1 tablespoon finely chopped tarragon
½ cup dry white wine
1 cup heavy cream
4 ounces (1 stick) butter, cubed
Kosher salt, to taste
Freshly ground white pepper, to taste
Cooked homemade pasta, to serve
  (see recipe on page 44)

1. Saute the shrimp in clarified butter in a hot pan until they are about a quarter of the way cooked.

2. Add the garlic and shallot and saute until the garlic begins to brown. Add the tarragon and toss for 10 seconds. Deglaze with white wine and reduce the wine by half.

3. Add the heavy cream and reduce the liquid until it has reached sauce consistency. Swirl in the butter cubes. Season the sauce with salt and pepper, to taste.

4. To serve, add the cooked homemade pasta and toss to coat it with the sauce. Serve on a hot plate.

Serves 4

technique.
Deglazing allows you to capture every bit of flavor from a protein that has been sauteed or panfried. The technique involves using a liquid such as wine or stock to dissolve the caramelized, stuck-on bits from the bottom of the pan.

technique.
To make clarified butter, melt 1 stick (¼ pound) unsalted butter in a heavy saucepan over low heat; remove the pan from the heat and let it stand for 5 minutes. Skim any foam from the top and pour the liquid that remains into a bowl; discard any solids in the bottom of the pan. Clarified butter has a much higher smoke point than whole butter. Clarifying 1 stick of butter will yield about 6 tablespoons clarified butter.

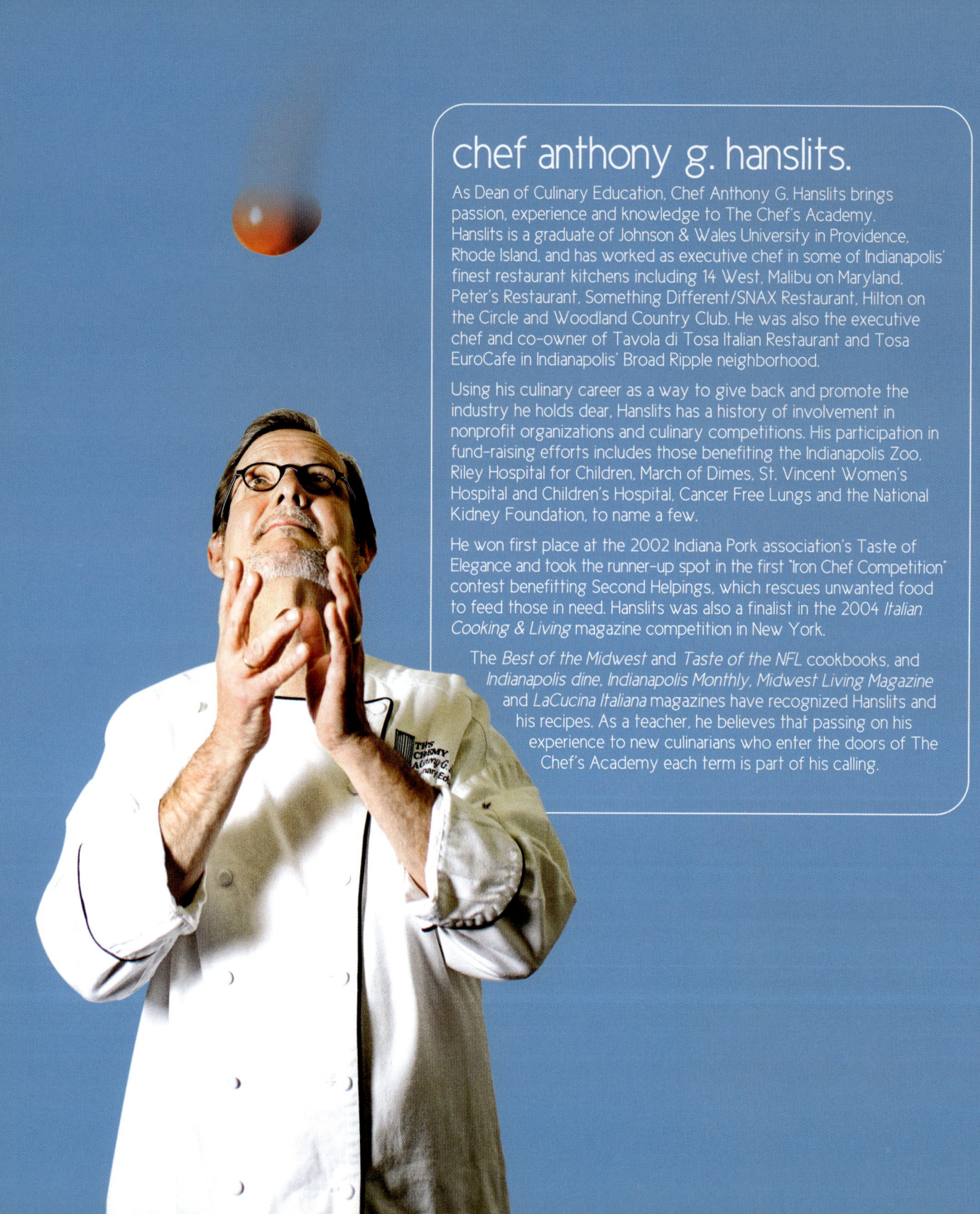

chef anthony g. hanslits.

As Dean of Culinary Education, Chef Anthony G. Hanslits brings passion, experience and knowledge to The Chef's Academy. Hanslits is a graduate of Johnson & Wales University in Providence, Rhode Island, and has worked as executive chef in some of Indianapolis' finest restaurant kitchens including 14 West, Malibu on Maryland, Peter's Restaurant, Something Different/SNAX Restaurant, Hilton on the Circle and Woodland Country Club. He was also the executive chef and co-owner of Tavola di Tosa Italian Restaurant and Tosa EuroCafe in Indianapolis' Broad Ripple neighborhood.

Using his culinary career as a way to give back and promote the industry he holds dear, Hanslits has a history of involvement in nonprofit organizations and culinary competitions. His participation in fund-raising efforts includes those benefiting the Indianapolis Zoo, Riley Hospital for Children, March of Dimes, St. Vincent Women's Hospital and Children's Hospital, Cancer Free Lungs and the National Kidney Foundation, to name a few.

He won first place at the 2002 Indiana Pork association's Taste of Elegance and took the runner-up spot in the first "Iron Chef Competition" contest benefitting Second Helpings, which rescues unwanted food to feed those in need. Hanslits was also a finalist in the 2004 *Italian Cooking & Living* magazine competition in New York.

The *Best of the Midwest* and *Taste of the NFL* cookbooks, and *Indianapolis dine*, *Indianapolis Monthly*, *Midwest Living Magazine* and *LaCucina Italiana* magazines have recognized Hanslits and his recipes. As a teacher, he believes that passing on his experience to new culinarians who enter the doors of The Chef's Academy each term is part of his calling.

poultry & pork

spicy chicken kebabs

Kebabs

4 boneless, skinless chicken breasts
1 red bell pepper
1 yellow onion

Marinade

1 teaspoon chili powder
1 teaspoon chopped garlic
1 teaspoon cumin
1 teaspoon chopped ginger
1 teaspoon ground coriander
1 teaspoon chopped rosemary
¼ teaspoon cayenne pepper
½ teaspoon kosher salt
½ teaspoon freshly ground black pepper
4 tablespoons grated or pureed onion
4 tablespoons vanilla yogurt
4 tablespoons lime juice

Sauce

½ cup vanilla yogurt
1 teaspoon chopped mint leaves
Lime juice, to taste
Kosher salt, to taste
Freshly ground black pepper, to taste

1. Soak 8 8-inch wooden skewers in water at least 1 hour (about 3 hours before serving).
2. Dice the chicken breasts, pepper and onion into ½- to 1-inch-square chunks. Thread them onto the skewers, alternating chicken, pepper and then onion, repeating until finished.
3. Combine all of the marinade ingredients in a mixing bowl and smear the mixture liberally over the kebabs. Cover them and refrigerate at least 2 hours.
4. While the kebabs are marinating, in a small mixing bowl, combine all of the sauce ingredients and refrigerate until service.
5. Preheat grill to medium-high and grill the kebabs to desired doneness.
6. Top the kebabs with the sauce and serve hot.

Serves 4 (2 skewers per person)

chicken tagine

BY CHEF ROBERT FRYE

- 2 teaspoons freshly ground white pepper
- 2 teaspoons ground coriander
- 2 teaspoons turmeric
- 2 teaspoons ground cumin
- 2 teaspoons curry powder
- ¼ cup extra-virgin olive oil
- 6 chicken thighs
- Salt, to taste
- Freshly ground black pepper, to taste
- 2 large onions, thinly sliced
- 2 heads garlic, cloves peeled and sliced
- 4 tablespoons chopped fresh ginger or ginger powder
- 4 tomatoes, peeled and seeded (see technique on page 69)
- 1 pint chicken stock
- 2 tablespoons slivered almonds, toasted (see technique on page 18)

1. In a spice grinder or blender, combine the white pepper, coriander, turmeric, cumin and curry powder.
2. Preheat an extra-large casserole over medium-high heat with the olive oil.
3. Season the thighs well with salt and pepper and then add them to the pan, skin side down, cooking until the skin is golden brown. Season with a little of the spice mix. Turn and brown the other side.
4. Add the rest of the spice mix, the onions, garlic, ginger and tomatoes to the pan and allow the vegetables to sweat.
5. Add the chicken stock and bring to a simmer. Cover and cook until the chicken is tender and cooked through. Garnish with toasted almonds.

Serves 6

tidbit.

Agriculture is big business in Indiana, from watermelon and duck to snap beans and peppermint. Corn was the leading source of income for Indiana farmers in 2007, followed by soybeans and meat animals. Poultry and eggs came in as the fourth-leading contributor with $811 million, followed by dairy. These five commodity groups accounted for over 91 percent of the 2007 cash receipts.

duck ragu and sweet corn "risotto"

BY CHEF ANTHONY G. HANSLITS

Duck Ragu

- ⅓ cup olive oil
- 4 duck leg quarters (drumstick and thigh), skinned
- Kosher salt, to taste
- Freshly ground black pepper, to taste
- 1 cup small-dice onion
- ½ cup medium-dice carrot
- 2 cloves garlic, thinly sliced
- 1 stalk celery, medium dice
- 2 teaspoons chopped sage
- 2 cups red wine
- 3 cups whole plum tomatoes, peeled (see technique on page 69)
- 1 cup veal stock

Sweet Corn "Risotto"

- 2 cups chicken broth
- 2 ounces (4 tablespoons) butter
- 1 cup diced onion
- 4 ears corn, kernels cut from the cob
- 1 cup fresh peas
- 1 cup heavy cream
- ¾ cup freshly grated Parmesan cheese
- Kosher salt, to taste
- Freshly ground black pepper, to taste

Duck Ragu

1. In a thick-bottomed pan, heat the olive oil until almost smoking over medium-high heat.
2. Season the duck with salt and pepper and cook in the skillet until brown on all sides. Remove the duck and set aside.
3. Add the onion, carrot, garlic, celery and sage to the pan. Reduce the heat to low and cook until soft (about 8 minutes). Add the wine, tomatoes and veal stock; bring to a boil.
4. Return the duck to the pan; reduce the heat, cover and simmer until the sauce has thickened (45 minutes–1 hour).
5. Remove the duck pieces from the pan. When they are cool enough to handle, pull all of the meat from the bones. Return the meat to the pan and simmer uncovered until the sauce has further thickened (30–45 minutes). Season, to taste, with salt and pepper.
6. Serve with Sweet Corn "Risotto." This also makes a great sauce for plain risotto or large pasta such as pappardelle.

Serves 8

Sweet Corn "Risotto"

1. In a saucepan over medium-high heat, bring the broth to a simmer.
2. In a large saute pan over medium heat, melt the butter. Add the onion and cook until translucent (about 5 minutes). Add the corn kernels and cook 1–2 more minutes.
3. Pour in ½ cup of the simmering broth, stirring constantly until the broth has been absorbed. Continue to add the broth about ½ cup at a time. With the third addition of broth, add the peas. Keep adding broth until all of it has been used.
4. Add the cream and cook 1–2 more minutes.
5. Remove from heat and stir in the Parmesan cheese to incorporate. Season with salt and pepper, to taste. Serve with Duck Ragu.

Serves 4

tidbit.

Maple Leaf Farms in Milford, Indiana, is the leading producer of duck in the United States. The family-owned business was founded in 1958 and works with Amish and Mennonite farmers in the Midwest. Its White Pekin poultry, the most popular breed of duck eaten in the U.S., are fed a diet of corn, wheat and soybeans.

pork medallions with marsala, garlic and herbs

BY CHEF ANTHONY G. HANSLITS

2 tablespoons chopped rosemary
2 tablespoons chopped sage leaves
1 cup chopped basil leaves
6 cloves garlic, chopped
12 2-ounce pork medallions*
Kosher salt, to taste
Freshly ground black pepper, to taste
2 tablespoons extra-virgin olive oil
½ cup marsala wine
1 cup veal or chicken stock
4 tablespoons unsalted butter

1. Combine the rosemary, sage, basil and garlic in a mixing bowl.
2. Season the pork medallions with salt and pepper, to taste.
3. Heat a large saute pan over high heat.
4. Rub the medallions with the herb mixture.
5. Add the olive oil to the hot pan and place the herb-crusted pork medallions in the pan. Do not crowd the pork. If the pan is too small, you may have to cook them in 2 batches.
6. Saute the pork until medium doneness (about 3 minutes on each side) and then remove them from the pan.
7. Add the wine and stock to the pan, scraping the bottom to loosen any bits (see deglazing technique on page 53); bring to a simmer and reduce the sauce until it thickens. Remove from the heat and whisk in the butter 1 tablespoon at a time.
8. To serve, place 3 medallions on 4 separate plates. Divide the sauce evenly.

Serves 4

*You may also use 4 6-ounce slices of pork, like the portion shown in the photograph. Increase your cook time to ensure doneness.

tidbit.

Of all agricultural commodities produced in Indiana in 2007, hogs accounted for 10 percent of money made. As the eighth largest pork producer in the country, Indiana and its cooks aren't shy about their love of pork, from slices of juicy ham to strips of smoky bacon. The pork tenderloin sandwich is a state treasure, usually served breaded and fried with pickles, onions and mayonnaise.

garlic herb-encrusted pork loin

BY CHEF MATTHEW MEJIA

5 tablespoons olive oil
1½ cups bread crumbs
2 teaspoons finely chopped fresh rosemary
1 large clove garlic
2 pounds pork rack or boneless pork loin
1 teaspoon kosher salt
1 teaspoon freshly ground black pepper
2 tablespoons Dijon mustard

1. Preheat oven to 325 degrees.

2. Combine 4 tablespoons (¼ cup) of the olive oil, bread crumbs, rosemary and garlic in a food processor and blend until well combined. Be sure the garlic clove gets chopped up well.

3. Rinse off the pork and then pat it dry; season with salt and pepper.

4. In a skillet, heat the remaining 1 tablespoon oil over moderately high heat until it is hot but not smoking; brown the pork on all sides. Transfer the pork to a shallow baking pan and evenly coat the top and sides with the mustard. Evenly press the bread crumb mixture onto the mustard, entirely covering the meat.

5. Roast the pork in the middle of the 325-degree oven until a meat thermometer inserted into the center indicates 155 degrees. (It should take about 40 minutes-1 hour, depending on how done you want it.) (If the bread crumbs begin to get too browned, you may cover the pork loosely with foil.) Transfer the meat to a cutting board and let it stand 5 minutes before slicing. (This helps to retain the juices.)

Serves 4-6

butter "poached" pork loin with warm onion marmalade

BY CHEF JEFFREY BANE

Butter "Poached" Pork Loin
- 6 cloves garlic, minced
- 3 tablespoons kosher salt
- 6 bay leaves
- 1¼ teaspoons all-purpose curing mix (pink salt*)
- 4 shallots, chopped
- 1 bunch Italian parsley
- 2 ounces rosemary leaves (about 2 stems)
- 5 pounds boneless pork loin
- Enough rendered pork lard and clarified butter to cover the meat†

Warm Onion Marmalade
- 20 black peppercorns
- 6 large onions, diced or very thinly sliced
- 3 cups sherry wine
- 1 cup strong veal stock
- 4 bay leaves
- 6 juniper berries
- 8 ounces dried plums, medium dice
- 1 teaspoon chopped parsley
- 1 teaspoon chopped rosemary
- Kosher salt, to taste
- Freshly ground black pepper, to taste

Butter "Poached" Pork Loin

1. Two days before serving, combine the garlic, salt, bay leaves, pink salt, shallots, parsley and rosemary in a food processor and blend well to completely chop the herbs.
2. Rub this mixture into the meat and store in a plastic or nonreactive container in the refrigerator for 48 hours.
3. Preheat oven to 180 degrees.
4. In an ovenproof pan large enough to hold the pork, heat the rendered lard and clarified butter to 180 degrees on the stovetop.
5. Rinse all of the marinade mixture off of the pork and pat dry. Completely submerge the pork in the fat and simmer gently for 20 minutes.
6. Place in the 180-degree oven, uncovered, until the pork is completely tender and cooked through (about 6 hours).
7. Once it is tender, the pork can be cooled in the same fat; if sealed off from the air, it will last for over 3 weeks. Confit can be eaten at room temperature or heated. Serve with Warm Onion Marmalade.

Serves 10

*Pink curing salt contains nitrates to "cure" the meat.

†Purchase rendered pork lard from a trusted butcher. I get mine from Claus' German Sausage & Meats in downtown Indianapolis. (For clarified butter, see technique on page 53.)

Warm Onion Marmalade

1. Put the peppercorns on a small piece of cheesecloth, gather the ends and tie to secure.
2. Place the sachet, onions, sherry, stock, bay leaves and juniper berries in a stainless-steel, thick-bottomed saucepan and simmer the mixture on very low heat until almost all of the liquid is evaporated and the onions are translucent. They should be sweet in flavor.
3. Remove the peppercorns and juniper berries from the pan. Fold in the plums, parsley and rosemary while the mixture is still hot; adjust seasonings with salt and pepper, to taste.

Serves 12

technique.

Bundling herbs or whole spices in cheesecloth to make a sachet or with kitchen string, as in a bouquet garni, allows you to control how intensely a dish is flavored – they can be removed at any time. It also eliminates any unwanted herbs or whole seeds from the finished product.

chef lucas trinosky.

Chef Lucas Trinosky has been cooking professionally since he graduated from culinary school in 1995, but his affection for food began much earlier. As a boy, instead of Spider Man and Popeye, his Saturday morning heroes were *The Frugal Gourmet's* Jeff Smith, Martin Yan on *Yan Can Cook* and Julia Child.

He enrolled at Johnson and Wales University right after high school and earned an Associate's of Applied Science degree in Culinary Arts. Right after graduation, he moved to Cincinnati, Ohio, and took a position as a pantry cook at the Millennium Hotel. Within a year and a half, he was promoted to sous chef of a related property in Durham, North Carolina. Just two years in, he was promoted to executive chef. He returned to Ohio to be the executive sous chef for the Hyatt Regency Cincinnati.

While living and working in Cincinnati, he became good friends with a local Swiss baker and picked up a few hours a week learning the European style of breads and pastries. Six months later, Trinosky started full time at the independent shop, baking and providing catering services for private jets that flew in and out of Lunken Airport. Within a year, the two friends would open Jean Paul's Paradiso, a small pizzeria that served soups, salads, sandwiches and pastas — all from scratch. It was here that Trinosky learned what it takes to run a business. Moving back to his hometown of Van Wert, Ohio, he opened the Harvest Stone Bakery and Catering Co. and began consulting, catering, creating ice sculptures and baking for businesses and individuals in the area.

Trinosky has been with The Chef's Academy since its opening in September 2006 and has taught all of the kitchen classes. In addition, he spends time working with students who have interests in the art of fruit and vegetable carving and serves as the advisor for the Beer Brewing Club.

lamb & beef

lamb fricassee

BY CHEF ANTHONY G. HANSLITS

½ cup extra-virgin olive oil
¾ cup small-dice onion
½ cup medium-dice celery
1½ pounds leg of lamb meat, cut into 1-inch pieces
½ cup peeled, seeded and diced tomatoes
½ cup dry red wine
Water, as needed
2 teaspoons chopped rosemary
½ cup fresh peas
Kosher salt, to taste
Freshly ground black pepper, to taste
½ cup grated pecorino cheese
1 large egg

1. Heat the olive oil in a large frying pan over medium heat and add the onion and celery. Cook for 5 minutes, stirring often.
2. Add the lamb, tomatoes, red wine and just enough water to cover the lamb; simmer until the lamb is very tender (about 1 hour).
3. Preheat oven to 350 degrees.
4. When the lamb is almost done cooking, add the rosemary and continue cooking. In the meantime, in a saucepan, cover the peas with water seasoned with salt and pepper, to taste. Bring to a boil over high heat and cook the peas until they are tender (6–8 minutes).
5. Drain the peas and pour them into a gratin dish or Dutch oven. Add the lamb pieces to the dish, reserving the cooking liquid from the lamb. Mix the lamb and peas together and add 1 cup of the lamb cooking liquid to the dish.
6. In a small bowl, mix together the pecorino cheese and egg. Top the lamb mixture with the egg mixture.
7. Bake in the 350-degree oven for 20 minutes and serve.

Serves 4

technique.

To peel tomatoes, plunge them in boiling water until the skin begins to pull away from the meat. Run them under cold water and peel away. Use a spoon to scoop out the seeds before slicing or cutting as needed.

veal scaloppini with mozzarella

BY CHEF ANTHONY G. HANSLITS

12 2-ounce pieces veal, pounded thin (1½ pounds)
2 tablespoons all-purpose flour
1 tablespoon butter
4 tablespoons extra-virgin olive oil
4 ounces fresh mozzarella, sliced into 4 pieces
2 tomatoes, peeled, seeded and diced (see technique on page 69)
1 teaspoon chopped oregano
1 teaspoon chopped marjoram
Kosher salt, to taste
Freshly ground black pepper, to taste

1 Dredge the veal in the flour. Shake off any excess.

2 In a large skillet, heat the butter and 3 tablespoons of the olive oil over high heat. saute the veal for 30 seconds on 1 side.

3 Turn over the scaloppini and top with the mozzarella. With heat remaining on high, cover with a lid and cook until the cheese starts to melt. (Watch it carefully to avoid overcooking the meat.) Remove pan from heat and keep covered.

4 In another skillet, heat the remaining 1 tablespoon olive oil and saute the tomatoes. Season with the oregano, marjoram, and salt and pepper, to taste.

5 Plate the veal and top with the sauce.

Serves 4

filet of beef with oregano and garlic olive oil

BY CHEF ANTHONY G. HANSLITS

½ cup extra-virgin olive oil
1 clove garlic, sliced
2 teaspoons sea salt, plus more to taste
2 tablespoons roughly chopped oregano leaves
4 8- or 12-ounce beef filets
Freshly ground black pepper, to taste

1. Preheat grill to high heat (about 500 degrees).
2. In a small mixing bowl, combine the olive oil, garlic, salt and oregano.
3. Salt and pepper both sides of the filets. The thickness of the steak will determine the length of cooking time. For 8-ounce, medium-rare steaks, place on the grill and cook for 3 minutes. Rotate the steak 180 degrees and cook for another 3 minutes. (This will form a crisscross on the steak.) Turn over and repeat on the other side. You may check the temperature of the meat with a meat thermometer, looking for an internal temperature of 130 degrees.
4. Remove the steaks from the grill and brush on all sides with the olive oil mixture. Let them rest for 5 minutes and serve.

Serves 4

butter-burgers

BY CHEF LUCAS TRINOSKY

4 ounces (1 stick) butter plus 1 tablespoon butter
2 pounds ground chuck
1 onion
1 teaspoon kosher salt
½ teaspoon freshly ground black pepper
2 tablespoons heavy cream
1 tablespoon canola oil
8 kaiser buns
Condiments, to your liking

1. Using a hand mixer, whip the stick of butter until light and fluffy. Save to top the cooked burgers.
2. Preheat a cast-iron skillet over medium-high heat.
3. Spread out the beef on a cutting board. Finely grate 3 tablespoons of the onion over the beef. Sprinkle with the salt and pepper, and drizzle with cream.
4. Mix the meat by hand and pat into 8 4-ounce burgers.
5. Add the remaining 1 tablespoon butter and the oil to the skillet. Cook the burgers to medium-well; there should be a nice crust on each side of the meat (about 3-4 minutes per side).
6. Toast the buns if desired. Place each burger on a bottom bun and add 1 tablespoon of the whipped butter.
7. Finish burger with your favorite condiments.

Serves 8

tip.
Mix together 8 parts kosher salt and 1 part freshly ground pepper and keep it handy. When a recipe calls for "salt and pepper, to taste," this ratio is a great place to start.

chef joseph allford.

In the Pastry Arts program, Chef Instructor Joseph Allford brings real-world restaurant experience and a lifelong respect for sustainability and regionality to his teaching. Like so many chefs, the Wilkinson native didn't realize his place was in a professional kitchen when he began his postsecondary education. As a student at Indiana University in Bloomington, he took a class focusing on Reay Tannahill's *Food in History*, the classic book exploring how what we eat has forged our human story. Inspired by Tannahill's work and a part-time job at the Encore Café, Allford decided he was more suited to a career in food than his chosen course of studies in psychology and film.

Allford left I.U. and moved to Vermont to attend the two-year program at the New England Culinary Institute, which set the stage for traveling and cooking internationally. After an internship at Something Different in Indianapolis, Allford moved to County Sligo, Ireland, to work in the esteemed Cromleach Lodge country hotel. The experience became the pivotal point in his career, as he rose from commis chef to head chef de cuisine in a matter of two years. Spending time in patisseries and chocolate shops in Brussels, Cologne, London and Montreal opened the world of patisserie to him.

Upon returning to the United States, Allford worked in several of Indianapolis' top restaurants, including The Kendall Inn and Tavola di Tosa. On staff at Peterson's restaurant for four years, he created dessert menus influenced by his signature seasonality. *Indianapolis dine* and *Indianapolis Monthly* magazines, and *The Indianapolis Star* have recognized his award-winning talents. Since 2004, Allford has also been teaching culinary classes at Frasier's Gourmet Foods shop and providing clients across the United States with private catered events and wedding cakes. Allford joined The Chef's Academy in 2008.

desserts

coconut flan

BY CHEF MATTHEW MEJIA

Flan
14 ounces (1¾ cups) coconut milk
9 ounces heavy cream
4 whole eggs
10 egg yolks
1 cup sugar
2 teaspoons vanilla extract
2 teaspoons coconut extract

Caramel
2½ cups granulated sugar

To finish
Sweetened, shredded coconut, to garnish
12 mint sprigs, to garnish

Flan

1. Place all of the ingredients in a mixing bowl and combine thoroughly with a whisk. Put into a plastic container. Cover with a tightly sealing lid and refrigerate overnight or at least 2 hours to let the bubbles rise to the top. (This creates a smoother flan.)

Caramel

1. Melt the sugar in a saucepan over medium-high heat until it turns a light amber color.
2. Pour the caramel at least ¼-inch deep into 12 10-ounce ovenproof soup cups or slightly tapered ramekins at least 2 inches deep. Cover with plastic wrap and set aside until the flan mixture is ready.

To finish

1. Preheat oven to 325 degrees.
2. Gently fold the flan mixture together with a spatula. Pour it into the prepared soup cups up to ½ inch from the top. Place the cups in a deep baking pan and fill the pan with water to create a water bath. Bake the flan until it is firm (about 2 hours).
3. Cool the flan by removing the cups from the water bath, individually wrapping them in plastic and placing them in the refrigerator. Cool for at least 6 hours or overnight.
4. To serve, remove the plastic and carefully separate each flan from its cup by cutting around it with a paring knife. Invert the cup and place it on a plate. Be sure to pour all of the caramel on top as well.
5. Garnish with sweetened shredded coconut (toasted if you wish) and a sprig of mint.

Makes 12 10-ounce servings

tip.
A water bath promotes gentle, even baking as the hot water surrounding the food helps to cook it. This is especially important for egg-based dishes such as flans and custards.

cake and ice cream

BY CHEF JOSEPH ALLFORD

Basic Ice Cream
(without an ice cream machine)
- 3 cups heavy cream
- 1 vanilla bean, split and scraped
- 4 eggs
- 1 cup powdered sugar
- 2 ounces liquor such as vodka or rum

Coffee Ice Cream Variation
- 3 cups heavy cream
- 1 vanilla bean, split and scraped
- 4 tablespoons coarsely ground coffee
- 4 eggs
- 1 cup powdered sugar
- 4 tablespoons coffee liqueur

Chocolate Variation
- 4 ounces chocolate, finely chopped
- 3 cups heavy cream
- 1 vanilla bean, split and scraped
- 4 eggs
- 1 cup powdered sugar
- 2 ounces liquor such as vodka or rum

Strawberry Variation
- 3 cups heavy cream
- 1 vanilla bean, split and scraped
- 4 eggs
- 1 cup powdered sugar
- 2 ounces liquor such as vodka or rum
- 4 ounces strawberry jam

Basic Ice Cream (without an ice cream machine)

1. Scald $1/2$ cup of the cream with the vanilla bean. Set aside to cool.
2. Whip the eggs with the sugar until they are light and fluffy.
3. Fold the vodka or rum and scalded cream into the egg mixture.
4. Whip the remaining $2 1/2$ cups cream to stiff peaks. Fold the egg mixture into the cream.
5. Freeze the ice cream overnight or for at least 6 hours.

Yields 2 quarts

Coffee Ice Cream Variation

1. Scald $1/2$ cup of the cream with the vanilla bean and coffee grounds. Set aside to cool.
2. Whip the eggs with the sugar until they are light and fluffy.
3. Fold the liqueur and scalded cream into the egg mixture.
4. Whip the remaining $2 1/2$ cups cream to stiff peaks. Fold the egg mixture into the cream.
5. Freeze the ice cream overnight or for at least 6 hours.

Yields 2 quarts

Chocolate Variation

1. Melt the chocolate chips.
2. Scald $1/2$ cup of the cream with the vanilla bean. Stir in the chocolate. Set aside to cool.
3. Whip the eggs with the sugar until they are light and fluffy.
4. Fold the vodka or rum and scalded cream into the egg mixture.
5. Whip the remaining $2 1/2$ cups cream to stiff peaks. Fold the egg mixture into the cream.
6. Freeze the ice cream overnight or for at least 6 hours.

Yields 2 quarts

Strawberry Variation

1. Scald $1/2$ cup of the cream with the vanilla bean. Set aside to cool.
2. Whip the eggs with the sugar until they are light and fluffy.
3. Fold the vodka or rum and scalded cream into the egg mixture. Fold the strawberry jam into the egg mixture.
4. Whip the remaining $2 1/2$ cups cream to stiff peaks. Fold the egg mixture into the cream.
5. Freeze the ice cream overnight or for at least 6 hours.

Yields 2 quarts

tip.
In many custard or flavored-cream recipes, scalding the cream or milk at 180 degrees allows the lactase to start caramelizing, changing its flavor profile to become malt-like, almost sweeter. Also, 180 degrees is the temperature at which flavors most readily attach themselves – on a molecular level – to fatty molecules. Therefore, vanilla-scented heavy cream is at its most vanilla-like when heated to 180 degrees. When it comes to bread or grain-based recipes, the process of scalding deadens an enzyme present in most dairy products that would otherwise devour many of the starches.

Pound Cake
- 1 cup unsalted butter, softened, plus more for prepping baking tin
- 1¼ cups plus 4 ounces granulated sugar
- ½ teaspoon kosher salt
- 3 eggs
- 3 egg yolks
- 1 teaspoon vanilla extract
- 1 tablespoon plus ½ cup water
- 1¼ cups all-purpose flour

Pound Cake

1. Grease parchment paper and use it to line a baking tin or loaf tin. Preheat oven to 350 degrees.
2. Cream the butter, 1¼ cups of the sugar and salt in an electric mixer with the whip attachment for several minutes until the mixture is light and fluffy.
3. Add the eggs and egg yolks to the creamed butter and continue whipping for several minutes until the mixture is smooth.
4. Add the vanilla extract and 1 tablespoon of the water to the mixture and combine.
5. Sift the flour into the butter mixture and fold together.
6. Bake the cake in the prepared baking tin at 350 degrees until it is well browned and a knife inserted into the center comes out clean (25-35 minutes).
7. While the cake is baking, make sugar syrup by bringing the remaining ½ cup water and remaining 4 ounces sugar to a simmer. Remove the cake from the pan and immediately pour the sugar syrup over the cake when it comes out of the oven.
8. Cool the cake on a rack and serve with ice cream. (This pound cake can be wrapped and stored at room temperature for up to 1 week.)

Yields 1 1-pound loaf

tidbit.
More than 120 million gallons of ice cream and related products were produced in Indiana in 2007, second only in the nation to California.

pear and persimmon tart

BY CHEF JOSEPH ALLFORD

1. Prepare the dough in a food processor. Pulse the butter, sugar, salt, egg yolk and vanilla together until combined. Add the flour and pulse until the dough begins to come together. Once assembled, the tart dough can be covered with plastic wrap and refrigerated for 20 minutes before using.

2. Prepare the filling by tossing the sliced pears with half of the sugar and all of the lemon juice. Combine the remaining sugar with the persimmon pulp and vanilla.

3. Preheat oven to 375 degrees.

4. To assemble the tart, on a piece of floured parchment paper, roll out the tart dough to about ³⁄₈-inch thickness. Try to keep the dough in a round shape while rolling it out.

5. Spread the persimmon filling in the center of the dough, leaving about 2 inches of the edge exposed, and layer the pear slices over the persimmon filling. Turn up the edges of the tart dough to enclose the filling, just enough to hold it together; dot the top of the tart with the unsalted butter.*

6. Bake the tart in the 375-degree oven (preferably on a hearthstone) until the filling is bubbly and the edges are well browned (25-35 minutes).

7. Remove the tart after baking and allow it to cool. Serve it slightly warm or at room temperature with crème anglaise, ice cream or whipped cream.

Yields 1 9-inch tart

*You may also completely enclose the tart, like a fruit pie, as shown in the photo.

Tart Dough

- 8 tablespoons unsalted butter
- ¼ cup powdered sugar
- ¼ teaspoon kosher salt
- 1 egg yolk
- 1 teaspoon vanilla extract
- 1⅓ cups whole wheat flour, plus more for prepping parchment paper

Filling

- 2 large pears, cored and cut into ¼-inch-thick slices
- ¾ cup granulated sugar
- 1 tablespoon lemon juice
- 1 cup persimmon pulp
- 1 tablespoon vanilla extract
- 4 tablespoons unsalted butter
- Crème anglaise, ice cream or whipped cream, to serve

tidbit.

The American persimmon is known for its tragically fragile skin and astringency when harvested too early. But ripe persimmon pulp is incomparably sweet and delicious. In Indiana, this persnickety fruit is most often purchased frozen and goes into autumnal persimmon puddings.

sweet potato tart

BY CHEF LUCAS TRINOSKY

2 medium-size sweet potatoes
2 tablespoons pastry flour
¾ teaspoon cinnamon
⅛ teaspoon nutmeg
⅛ teaspoon ground ginger
1 pinch cloves
½ teaspoon kosher salt
3 tablespoons brown sugar
2 egg yolks
2 tablespoons heavy cream
4 4-inch pie shells
Chopped walnuts or pecans, to garnish (optional)

1. Preheat oven to 400 degrees. Bake the potatoes directly on the rack in the 400-degree oven until just fork tender (about 45 minutes). Let them cool slightly, peel and puree using a potato ricer or in a food processor.

2. Lower oven temperature to 350 degrees.

3. Sift the dry ingredients (flour, cinnamon, nutmeg, ginger, cloves, salt and brown sugar) and add to 1½ cups of the potato puree. Mix by hand to combine well.

4. In a separate bowl, using a hand mixer, mix the yolks and cream for about 30 seconds. Fold the yolk mixture into the potato mixture until it is smooth.

5. Pipe the puree using a star tip into 4 individual-size pie shells and bake in the 350-degree oven until browned on top (8-10 minutes).

6. You may top the cooked tarts with chopped walnuts or pecans if preferred.

Serves 4

chocolate soufflé with crème anglaise

BY CHEF JOSEPH ALLFORD

Chocolate Soufflé

- 7 ounces bittersweet chocolate, chopped
- ⅓ cup espresso or strong coffee
- 4 tablespoons unsalted butter, plus more for prepping dishes
- ⅓ cup all-purpose flour
- 2 cups whole milk
- 1 tablespoon vanilla extract
- 4 egg yolks
- 6 egg whites
- ⅛ teaspoon kosher salt
- ½ cup granulated sugar, plus more for prepping dishes
- Hot water, as needed

Crème Anglaise

- 1 cup whole milk
- 1 vanilla bean, split and scraped
- 2 egg yolks
- 4 tablespoons granulated sugar
- 1 teaspoon liqueur or vanilla extract

Chocolate Soufflé

1. Preheat oven to 425 degrees.
2. Prepare 6–8 soufflé dishes by spreading soft butter on the bottoms and sides of the dishes and coating them with granulated sugar, being sure to leave the top rim of the dishes clean.
3. Melt the chocolate and coffee together over a hot water bath (a heatproof mixing bowl set over a pot of simmering water). Remove from heat and keep nearby.
4. In a saucepan over medium heat, melt the 4 tablespoons butter and then whisk in the flour until combined. Add the milk to the flour mixture and whisk until simmering for 1–2 minutes; remove from heat. Continue stirring the mixture until it has cooled slightly. Stir in the vanilla and egg yolks. Add the chocolate mixture, combine well and reserve.
5. Whip the egg whites with the salt on medium speed for 1 minute until foamy. Increase the speed to high and whip the whites until soft peaks begin to form. Slowly add the sugar and continue whipping the whites until stiff peaks form. Fold ⅓ of the meringue into the chocolate mixture and then fold in the remaining meringue.
6. Fill each prepared dish ¾ full with the soufflé mixture. Smooth the top of each soufflé and place into a deep baking dish. Place the baking dish into the 425-degree oven and fill it with hot water until the water reaches halfway up the sides of the soufflé dishes (see tip on page 77). Decrease the temperature of the oven to 375 degrees and bake the soufflés 25–35 minutes, depending on the size of the dishes. Remove the soufflés from the oven when they have risen completely and serve immediately with crème anglaise.

Yields 6–8 portions

Crème Anglaise

1. In a saucepan, prepare a hot water bath over high heat.
2. Scald the milk and whole vanilla bean in a separate saucepan (see tip on page 79).
3. While the milk is coming up to temperature, whisk together the egg yolks and granulated sugar in a heatproof mixing bowl. When the milk just begins to simmer, slowly add it to the yolk mixture while stirring. Place the mixture over the hot water bath and continue stirring until the mixture has thickened; add the liqueur or vanilla extract and pour through a fine-mesh strainer. Cool and refrigerate the anglaise until service.

Yield 1½ cups

chef pierre giacometti.

Chef Pierre Giacometti grew up in the Principality of Monaco. His father was born in the town of Bergamo, Italy, at the foothills of the Alps, and his mother's home was Villefranche-sur-Mer, located near Nice on the sun-drenched French Riviera. With a family tree that represents some of the world's most acclaimed origins for breads and desserts, Giacometti started his culinary career working for one of the finest pastry shops in Monaco.

Giacometti graduated from the French Culinary Institute in Nice and took advanced courses at culinary institute LeNôtre Paris. In 1986, Giacometti moved to America where he has worked for three major corporations. His last position of 15 years was with Marsh Supermarkets in Indianapolis, where he developed a French pastry program. He is now a Pastry Chef Instructor at The Chef's Academy. The quality of his work reflects his understanding, passion and love for the art of pastries.

breads

apple brioche

BY CHEF JOSEPH ALLFORD

Sponge
1 cup bread flour
2 teaspoons dry active yeast
1 cup applesauce, room temperature
¼ cup whole milk, room temperature

Dough
3 eggs, room temperature
2 teaspoons kosher salt
2½ cups bread flour
⅓ cup whole wheat flour
1 cup unsalted butter, soft; plus melted butter for prepping

To finish
Vegetable oil or butter, for prepping
Melted unsalted butter, for brushing loaf
Thinly sliced apples, to garnish
Granulated sugar, to garnish
Applesauce, to garnish

1. In a mixing bowl, stir together the sponge ingredients until combined. Cover the bowl and let the sponge ferment at room temperature until very bubbly (30–45 minutes).

2. To make the dough, add the eggs and salt to the sponge and stir until combined; add the flours and mix on low until combined. Let the dough rest for 5 minutes. Meanwhile, use melted butter to grease a bowl or pan large enough to hold the dough.

3. Continue mixing on medium-low speed, slowly adding the 1 cup butter in 1-ounce pieces; allow each piece to fully incorporate into the dough before the next one is added. Once all of the butter has been added, continue mixing the dough until it is smooth, shiny and elastic (5–7 minutes).

4. Place the dough in the oiled container, cover with plastic wrap and place in the refrigerator for at least 4 hours or overnight.

5. Remove the dough from the refrigerator and shape it into 6 7-ounce portions while it is still chilled.

6. To finish, grease a loaf tin with vegetable oil or butter. Place 3 of the dough pieces into the greased loaf tin. In the center of each dough ball, make an indentation and place 1 tablespoon of the applesauce in it.

7. Place the remaining 3 dough balls on top of the ones in the loaf tin. Brush the loaf with melted butter and layer thin apple slices over the dough in a single layer. Cover the brioche with plastic wrap and let it proof until it has doubled in size (1–2 hours).

8. Preheat oven to 350 degrees.

9. Garnish the brioche with more apple slices and sprinkle with sugar. Bake the brioche in the 350-degree oven for 20 minutes. Lower the oven temperature to 325 degrees and continue baking until the internal temperature of the loaf is 180–190 degrees (25–35 minutes).

10. Remove the loaf from the baking pan and cool on a wire wrack. If serving immediately, garnish the brioche with applesauce. (To store, wrap the brioche tightly in plastic wrap and keep at room temperature 2–4 days or freeze for up to 1 month.)

Yields 1 2-pound loaf

raisin bread

BY CHEF PIERRE GIACOMETTI

Yeast Mixture
⅓ ounce dry active yeast
About ½ cup warm water (105-110 degrees)

Dough
1 ounce (2 tablespoons) unsalted butter, room temperature, plus more melted butter for prepping pan
1 cup warm milk (105-115 degrees)
1½ teaspoons kosher salt
3 ounces (6 tablespoons) honey
12 ounces bread flour (a digital scale works best for weighing)
6 ounces dark raisins
1 teaspoon cinnamon

To finish
1 egg
¼ cup milk
1 pinch kosher salt
Cinnamon and sugar mix, to taste

Yeast Mixture

1. Dissolve the dry active yeast in 1½ ounces (3 tablespoons) of the warm water. Combine the rest of the water with the dissolved yeast.

Dough

1. Brush the inside of 2 bread pans with melted butter.
2. Mix the yeast mixture with the warm milk, salt, honey and bread flour on medium speed until the dough is smooth and soft (8-10 minutes).
3. Add the raisins and cinnamon; mix another 2 minutes on low speed.
4. Cover the dough with plastic wrap and let it sit at room temperature for 45 minutes to ferment.
5. Divide the dough into 2 loaves and flatten out each into oval shapes.

To finish

1. Roll each oval back into a loaf shape.
2. Mix up an egg wash using the egg, milk and salt. Brush each loaf with the egg wash and sprinkle with the cinnamon and sugar mix, to taste. Spray the bread lightly with cooking spray and cover with a damp cloth. Let the loaves rise in a warm place until they have nearly doubled in volume.
3. Preheat oven to 375 degrees. Place the loaves into greased pans.
4. Bake in the 375-degree oven for 40 minutes. When the bread is done baking, it will be darker and have an internal temperature of 190-200 degrees. Unmold the bread and allow the loaves to cool on racks.

Yields 2 loaves

mediterranean olive bread

BY CHEF PIERRE GIACOMETTI

Yeast Mixture
¾ ounce (1½ tablespoons) dry active yeast
½ cup warm water (105-115 degrees)
½ tablespoon sugar
5 ounces (1 cup) bread flour

Dough
1 cup warm water (105-115 degrees)
3 tablespoons olive oil, plus more as needed
2 tablespoons granulated sugar
1 tablespoon kosher salt
2 cups bread flour
2 tablespoons chopped fresh thyme
1½ cups kalamata olives, pitted
Coarse salt, as needed

1. Mix up all of the yeast mixture ingredients; add this to all of the dough ingredients except for the kalamata olives and coarse salt.

2. Using a stand mixer, mix the dough until it is smooth and elastic (8-10 minutes on medium speed). Add the olives and mix 2 minutes on low speed.

3. Let the dough ferment, covered with a damp cloth, for 40 minutes.

4. Divide the dough into 2 equal pieces. Pinch them down and shape them into oval loaves. Let the loaves rise, covered with plastic wrap or a damp cloth, until they are 1½ times their original size.

5. Preheat oven to 375 degrees.

6. Brush the loaves with olive oil and sprinkle with the coarse salt. Bake on a sheet pan in the 375-degree oven for 35 minutes. Remove them from the oven and allow them to cool completely on a rack.

Yields 2 loaves

three-strand braids

BY CHEF PIERRE GIACOMETTI

Yeast Mixture
.4 ounce dry active yeast
10½ ounces (1⅓ cups) warm water (105-110 degrees)

Dough
1 pound and 5 ounces bread flour
.4 ounce kosher salt, plus 1 pinch salt for egg wash
2 ounces sugar
1 ounce nonfat solids milk (powdered milk)
1 ounce shortening
1 ounce butter
2 ounces egg, plus more for egg wash
¼ cup milk
Cinnamon and sugar mix, to taste

1 Dissolve the dry active yeast in 1½ ounces (3 tablespoons) of the water. Combine the rest of the water with the dissolved yeast. In the bowl of an electric mixer, combine the yeast mixture with all of the dough ingredients except milk and cinnamon and sugar mix at second or medium speed 10-12 minutes. It should be soft and elastic.

2 Allow the dough to ferment for 1½ hours at 80 degrees.*

3 Preheat oven to 375 degrees.

4 After fermentation, divide the dough into 3 6-ounce sections and roll each into a 1-foot-long rope. Lay the 3 strands side by side with a couple of inches between them.

5 Starting in the middle of the strands, fold the left strand over the center (1 over 2). Fold the right strand over the center (3 over 1). Repeat sequence to create a braid. When you reach the ends of the strands, turn the braid over and braid the other half. If desired, a smaller 3-strand braid can be placed on top.

6 Mix some egg with ¼ cup milk and a pinch salt; brush the loaf with the egg wash. Sprinkle with the cinnamon/sugar mix, to taste.

7 Bake on a sheet pan lined with parchment paper in the 375-degree oven for 25 minutes. The loaf will be golden when it is finished baking.

Yields 1 loaf

*Fermentation is a part of proofing, which is the process of granting the dough the time it needs to react and rest. While professional bread makers have proofing boxes, home cooks can recreate the tool at home. Boil a large saucepan full of water and place it in the bottom of your oven. This will create a "steam box" of sorts to soften the dough. You can also proof by simply covering prepared dough with a wet towel for several hours. A loaf of bread is proofed when it bounces back after you touch it.

fresh whole wheat pita bread

BY CHEF ROBERT FRYE

2¼ teaspoons dry active yeast
2½ cups warm water
1 pound bread flour
1 pound whole wheat flour
1 tablespoon kosher salt
1½ tablespoons olive oil

1. Combine the yeast and warm water, mixing well.
2. Add the flours and salt. Mix the dough on low speed until it is quite elastic (3–4 minutes).
3. Place the dough in a large bowl, brush it with the olive oil and then cover with plastic wrap; allow it to double in size (1–2 hours). Punch the dough down.
4. Scale the dough into 8 pieces. Allow each dough section to double in size before rolling.
5. Preheat oven to 450 degrees. Dust a workspace with flour. Roll each pita into a disc about 7 inches in diameter. Rest and relax the dough for 10 minutes.
6. Bake on a sheet pan or pizza stone in the 450-degree oven until golden brown and puffed (4–8 minutes).

Yields 8 pita

techniques, tidbits and tips

Blanching, 28
Chiffonade, 25
Clarifying butter, 53
Deglazing, 53
Herb sachet, 65
Indiana agriculture, 59
Indiana corn, 35
Indiana duck, 61
Indiana ice cream, 79
Indiana pork, 62
Julienne, 50
Mangoes, 21
Peeling tomatoes, 69
Persimmons, 80
Reconstituting chili peppers, 20
Roasting bell peppers, 43
Saffron, 51
Salt and pepper mix, 73
Scalding milk, 79
Slicing soft cheese, 25
Stocks, 51
Toasting nuts, 18
Water bath, 77

chef instructors

Allford, Joseph, 74
Bane, Jeffrey, 8
Bright, Scott, 22
Frye, Robert, 30
Giacometti, Pierre, 84
Hanslits, Anthony G., 54
Mejia, Matthew, 40
Trinosky, Lucas, 66

recipes

APPETIZERS, 9
Bacalao with Aïoli, 12
Cazuela de Pollo con Chorizo y Hongos, 13
Chipotle Lime Salsa, 20
Crispelle (Tiny Fried Pizza), 15
Hummus, 16
Jalapeño Pesto, 17
Kohlrabi with Red and Yellow Beets, Roasted, 11
Mango Salsa, 21
Mint and Pistachio Pesto, 18
Sun-Dried Tomato Tapenade, 19

Apple Brioche, 87
Bacalao with Aïoli, 12
Beer and Cheddar Soup, 38

BREADS, 85
Apple Brioche, 87
Mediterranean Olive Bread, 89
Raisin Bread, 88
Three-Strand Braids, 90
Whole Wheat Pita Bread, Fresh, 91

Butter-Burgers, 73
Cake and Ice Cream, 78
Cazuela de Pollo con Chorizo y Hongos, 13
Chicken Kebabs, Spicy, 57
Chicken Tagine, 59
Chipotle Lime Salsa, 20
Chocolate Soufflé with Crème Anglaise, 83
Coconut Flan, 77
Corn Chowder, 35
Crispelle (Tiny Fried Pizza), 15

DESSERTS, 75
Cake and Ice Cream, 78
Chocolate Soufflé with Crème Anglaise, 83
Coconut Flan, 77
Pear and Persimmon Tart, 80
Sweet Potato Tart, 81

Duck Ragu and Sweet Corn "Risotto," 61
English Claiborne, 47
Filet of Beef with Oregano and Garlic Olive Oil, 71
Gazpacho Blanco, 33
Green Bean and Fontina Salad, 25
Grilled Swordfish with Tabasco Anchovy Sauce and Sun-Dried Tomatoes, 50
Hummus, 16
Jalapeño Pesto, 17
Kohlrabi with Red and Yellow Beets, Roasted, 11

LAMB & BEEF, 67
Butter-Burgers, 73
Filet of Beef with Oregano and Garlic Olive Oil, 71
Lamb Fricassee, 69
Veal Scaloppini with Mozzarella, 70

Lamb Fricassee, 69
Mango Salsa, 21
Mediterranean Olive Bread, 89
Mint and Pistachio Pesto, 18
Octopus Salad, Baby, 27
Paddlefish Fajitas, 49
Pasta Dough, Egg, 44
Pear and Persimmon Tart, 80
Pork Loin, Garlic Herb-Encrusted, 63
Pork Loin with Warm Onion Marmalade, Butter "Poached," 65
Pork Medallions with Marsala, Garlic and Herbs, 62

POULTRY & PORK, 55
    Chicken Kebabs, Spicy, 57
    Chicken Tagine, 59
    Duck Ragu and Sweet Corn "Risotto," 61
    Pork Loin, Garlic Herb-Encrusted, 63
    Pork Loin with Warm Onion Marmalade, Butter "Poached," 65
    Pork Medallions with Marsala, Garlic and Herbs, 62

Provençal White Bean Soup, 36
Pumpkin Velouté with Serrano Ham and Dates, 37
(Rabbit Stew), Estofado de Conejo, 39
Raisin Bread, 88
Rhubarb Soup; Cool, Refreshing, 32
Roasted Portobello and Spinach Couscous Wrap, 46
Rock Shrimp (Langoustines) with Tarragon Cream Sauce, 53
Saffron Mussels with Ham, Peppers and Tomatoes, 51

SALADS, 23
    Green Bean and Fontina Salad, 25
    Octopus Salad, Baby, 27
    Seafood Salad, Spanish, 28
    Vegetable Salad, Grilled, 29

Seafood Salad, Spanish, 28

SOUPS, 31
    Beer and Cheddar Soup, 38
    Corn Chowder, 35
    Gazpacho Blanco, 33
    Provençal White Bean Soup, 36
    Pumpkin Velouté with Serrano Ham and Dates, 37
    (Rabbit Stew), Estofado de Conejo, 39
    Rhubarb Soup; Cool, Refreshing, 32

Stuffed Peppers with Tomato Vinaigrette, 43
Sun-Dried Tomato Mushroom Ravioli, 45
Sun-Dried Tomato Tapenade, 19
Sweet Potato Tart, 81
Three-Strand Braids, 90
Veal Scaloppini with Mozzarella, 70
Vegetable Salad, Grilled, 29

VEGETABLES & SEAFOOD, 41
    English Claiborne, 47
    Grilled Swordfish with Tabasco Anchovy Sauce and Sun-Dried Tomatoes, 50
    Paddlefish Fajitas, 49
    Pasta Dough, Egg, 44
    Roasted Portobello and Spinach Couscous Wrap, 46
    Rock Shrimp (Langoustines) with Tarragon Cream Sauce, 53
    Saffron Mussels with Ham, Peppers and Tomatoes, 51
    Stuffed Peppers with Tomato Vinaigrette, 43
    Sun-Dried Tomato Mushroom Ravioli, 45

Whole Wheat Pita Bread, Fresh, 91

the chef's academy

The Chef's Academy is the first dedicated campus in Indiana to focus solely on training the chefs of the future. Under the direction of Chef Anthony G. Hanslits, Dean of Culinary Education, students participate in career-focused classes in state-of-the-art kitchens, preparing them to be positive impacts on the hospitality industry upon graduation.

All students are required to complete internships and externships to gain first-hand experience in the culinary and hospitality industries. The Chef's Academy offers Associate's Degrees in Culinary or Pastry Arts and a Bachelor's Degree in Hospitality and Restaurant Management with classes starting five times a year.

The Chef's Academy is the Culinary Division of Harrison College, formerly Indiana Business College. Harrison College is a nationally accredited institution dedicated to excellence in higher learning. Harrison provides contemporary career education in a learning environment where students receive individualized support, care and respect.

Visit chefsacademy.com for more information.